Steck Vaughn

Social Studies

Teacher's Guide
Level C

Living IN OUR Communities

Harcourt Achieve
Rigby • Saxon • Steck-Vaughn

www.HarcourtAchieve.com
1.800.531.5015

ISBN 978-0-7398-9232-9

© 2005 Harcourt Achieve Inc.

All rights reserved. Harcourt Achieve Inc. grants permission to duplicate enough copies of the reproducible pages to distribute to students. Other than these specifically allowed pages, no part of the material protected by this copyright may be reproduced or utilized in any form or by any means, in whole or in part, without permission in writing from the copyright owner. Requests for permission should be mailed to: Copyright Permissions, Harcourt Achieve Inc., P.O. Box 27010, Austin, Texas 78755.

Rigby and Steck-Vaughn are trademarks of Harcourt Achieve Inc. registered in the United States of America and/or other jurisdictions.
Printed in the United States of America
11 2266 18
4500734442

ACKNOWLEDGMENTS

Executive Editor: Diane Sharpe
Project Editor: Janet Jerzycki
Assistant Art Director: Cynthia Ellis
Design Manager: John J. Harrison

Contents

Program Philosophy 4

Content Scope and Sequence 6

Skills Scope and Sequence 8

Teaching Strategies
   Unit 1 9
      Chapter 1 10
      Chapter 2 12
   Unit 2 14
      Chapter 3 15
      Chapter 4 17
      Chapter 5 19
      Chapter 6 21
   Unit 3 23
      Chapter 7 24
      Chapter 8 26
      Mid-Term Test (Units 1–3) 28
   Unit 4 30
      Chapter 9 31
      Chapter 10 33
      Chapter 11 35
   Unit 5 37
      Chapter 12 38
      Chapter 13 40
      Chapter 14 42
   Unit 6 44
      Chapter 15 45
      Chapter 16 47
      Final Test (Units 1–6) 49

Letters to Families
   Unit 1 51
   Unit 2 53
   Unit 3 55
   Unit 4 57
   Unit 5 59
   Unit 6 61

Graphic Organizers
   Concept Web 63
   Cause and Effect 64

The Philosophy of Steck-Vaughn Social Studies

Social studies focuses on developing knowledge and skill in history, geography, anthropology, economics, and political science. Most importantly, it focuses on people and their interaction with each other and the world in which they live. *Steck-Vaughn Social Studies* addresses these areas of study in a six-level program that correlates with the social studies curriculum throughout the United States. This program can serve as an alternative to traditional basal textbooks. *Steck-Vaughn Social Studies* helps students acquire the skills, knowledge, and understanding they must have in order to function as concerned and involved members of our society.

Steck-Vaughn Social Studies is a program that both you and your students will enjoy using. Its approach is based on widening the horizons of students as they progress through the elementary grades. Students will gain a concrete, understandable framework for learning the principles of democracy and citizenship. They will also gain a better vantage point from which to view the world's diversity.

ABOUT THE PUPIL EDITIONS

The individual features of *Steck-Vaughn Social Studies* have been designed to help students meet with success in their study of social studies. A variety of features work together to create books that are both inviting and manageable for students who have difficulty reading in this content area.

Format

The pupil texts are divided into units and chapters of manageable length. Each unit opener identifies the important concepts of the unit and sets the stage for successful reading by asking questions to spark student interest. A photograph welcomes students to each new unit. The unit opener also suggests an idea for an appealing cooperative learning project for students to carry out as they read the unit. The unit closes with suggestions of ways students can complete and present their project.

Interactive Activities

Activities on the pupil edition pages ensure student involvement by asking them to respond to the text. Many of the activities emphasize geography skills. Activities also include recall questions, higher-level thinking questions, and activities that require student interaction with maps, charts, and illustrations.

Readability

A readable and manageable text draws students into the content and ensures their understanding. The text never talks down to students or overwhelms them, but rather respects them and presents the content in a form they will understand and enjoy. Difficult concepts are presented in a straightforward manner. The students' prior knowledge is used as a starting point for presenting new concepts. The reading level is carefully controlled at or below grade level in order to ease the difficulties students often have with reading content-area materials.

Text	Reading Level
Level A	Grade 1
Level B	Grade 2
Level C	Grade 2
Level D	Grade 3
Level E	Grade 3
Level F	Grade 4

Vocabulary

Key social studies terms are boldfaced and defined in context in the texts. The glossary at the end of each book lists the terms and their definitions alphabetically.

Special Feature Pages

These pages appear at the end of every chapter and focus on a person, place, or event that extends the chapter content. For example, "Around the Globe" special features in Level C take students to Australia and Canada. In the chapter about ancient Egypt in Level F, the "Special People" feature focuses on Hatshepsut. One "For Your Information" in Level E extends the content of the Civil War with a description of the Freedmen's Bureau set up to help African Americans after the war.

History Strand

Steck-Vaughn Social Studies addresses the often neglected need for history in the lower grades. For example, students at Level A read about the first families in the United States—American Indians and Pilgrims. At Level C, students explore the development of a community—Omaha, Nebraska—from the days of the Omaha people to the present.

Skills Program

Each unit includes social studies and geography skills such as maps, globes, charts, and graphs as part of its narrative content. A Skill Builder at the end of each unit extends the content, at the same time reviewing a social studies or geography skill taught previously in the unit.

Maps and Illustrations

Students are drawn into the texts by abundant maps and illustrations that enhance their understanding of the content.

Chapter Checkups

Checkup tests provide successful closure to each chapter. The consistent format helps students feel comfortable in a review situation. Each Checkup consists of questions in standardized test format, which address the factual content of the chapter. A critical-thinking-and-writing question that requires students to display their deeper understanding of a chapter concept concludes the chapter.

ABOUT THE TEACHER'S GUIDE

The separate Teacher's Guide presents strategies for units and chapters with guidelines and answers for the interactive text; mid-term and final tests; letters to families; and useful graphic organizers.

Teaching Strategies

The unit strategies include a unit summary, pre- and post-reading activities, and guidelines for implementing the unit project. In addition, references to the Teacher's Resource Binder blacklines are included, should you choose to purchase this additional resource.

The chapter strategies include activities for pre- and post-reading, as well as a chapter summary, objectives, a list of vocabulary along with vocabulary activities, and page-by-page teaching suggestions and answers to interactive text.

These activities can help teachers accommodate the individual and group needs of students.

Letters to Families

Family letters are provided for every unit of Levels A, B, C, and D, and for each book of Levels E and F. The letters invite families to participate in their child's study of the book and provide suggestions for some specific activities that can extend the concepts. A separate Spanish version of each letter is also provided.

Assessment and Evaluation

A mid-term and final test are provided in the Teacher's Guides for Levels C, D, E, and F. The tests are in the standardized test format familiar to students from the Chapter Checkups.

To implement portfolio assessment, invite students to select samples of their best work to supply for their portfolios. Ask them to tell you which work they are most proud of and why. You may want to suggest that students' work on the cooperative learning unit projects be considered for their portfolios. Allow students to discuss with you any work they would like to change and how they would change it.

Meet your state standards with free blackline masters and links to other materials at www.HarcourtAchieve.com/AchievementZone. Click **Steck-Vaughn Standards**.

CONTENT SCOPE AND SEQUENCE

	LEVEL A	LEVEL B	LEVEL C
HISTORY	• People, families, and neighborhoods change over time. • American Indians were the first Americans. American Indians helped the Pilgrims to survive. • National holidays and patriotic symbols remind us of our heritage.	• American Indians were the first Americans. • Christopher Columbus came to America in search of new trade routes. • American Indians helped the Pilgrims survive in America. • Neighborhoods change over time. • Holidays commemorate special events and people from our history.	• American Indians made up our nation's earliest communities. • Pioneers settled on American Indian land and built communities such as Omaha, Nebraska. • Thanksgiving celebrates an event in American history. • Each community has its own history that we can research.
GEOGRAPHY	• Families live in homes of different sizes and shapes. • Different families need or want to live in different places (near rivers, mountains, etc.). • A globe is a model of Earth. • Earth provides us with many resources.	• Neighborhoods are real places we can show on maps. • Globes are ways of showing the whole, round Earth. • Neighborhoods around the world are both alike and different. • There are seven continents on Earth. • Earth has different geographic features such as mountains, plains, rivers, and oceans.	• Life in communities often depends on natural resources, climate, and landforms. • Water is a very valuable natural resource. • Plains and mountains are important landforms. • The American Indian way of life was shaped by the land.
GOVERNMENT/ CITIZENSHIP	• Rules help us to live, work, and play at home and in the community. • We have responsibilities in our families. • Families share feelings about their country and about their flag. • It is important to take care of the environment. • Families remember great Americans and events on special days.	• We live in the United States of America. • Neighbors work together to solve mutual problems. • Rules and laws tell us what to do and what not to do. Rules and laws help us live together. • Groups have leaders (mayor, governor, President).	• A community is run by a government • Government leaders are elected by the people of a community. • Communities have laws to tell people what to do and how to act, to protect people, and to provide safety. • Our national government is based in Washington, D.C.
ECONOMICS	• People work to earn money to buy the things they need and want. • Some people produce goods and others provide services. • We can't always have everything we want. People make choices as to which needs and wants they will satisfy.	• Some people produce goods and others provide services. • Workers cooperate to produce goods. • People use the money they earn to buy the things they need and want. • The choice of jobs may be limited by the place in which a person lives. • Taxes help pay for many community services.	• As workers, people are producers; as buyers, they are consumers. • One product may be produced by many people working in different communities. • Communities depend on one another. • Jobs and industry determine whether or not a community will grow or shrink.
SOCIOLOGY/ ANTHROPOLOGY	• Families vary in size and structure. • Families provide for physical and emotional needs and wants. Different families have somewhat different rules and private holidays. • Schools are special places for learning. • All family members can help the family meet its needs and wants.	• Neighborhoods are places in which to live, work, and play. • Neighbors vary in age, language, and other human characteristics. • People share the customs of their homelands with new friends and neighbors in the United States. • Neighbors share local and national holidays.	• Communities vary in size: rural towns, suburbs, and cities. • People live, work, and play in communities. • Living in communities makes it easier to get things done and to help people. • We have American traditions. • We also have many individual family traditions.

CONTENT SCOPE AND SEQUENCE

	LEVEL D	**LEVEL E**	**LEVEL F**
HISTORY	• The American Indians were the first to settle in what is now the U.S. • The U.S. has always been a nation of immigrants. • The geography and natural features of a region affect the course of its history.	• The history of the U.S. tells how different groups built a strong nation. • U.S. history can be divided into several distinct periods. • The study of these periods shows how people and events have shaped the present. • The study of the past shows the development of important ideas.	• Civilizations in Asia, Africa, Europe, and the Americas made key contributions to human life and knowledge. • The ancient Greeks and Romans and the nations of Western Europe have influenced many nations. • Geography, trade, and technology can affect the development of a civilization.
GEOGRAPHY	• The U.S. is a large nation. It includes 50 states and Puerto Rico. • The Northeast, Southeast, North Central, Rocky Mountain, Southwest, and Pacific regions are groups of states with characteristic geographic features. • Landforms and climate influence the way people live and work.	• The U.S. has diverse landforms, climates, and natural resources. • The U.S. can be divided into several distinct regions. • The geography of the U.S. has affected the ways in which the nation was explored and settled. • U.S. geography has influenced economic activities.	• Varied land regions, climates, resources, and bodies of water are found on Earth. • People adapt differently to different natural environments. • Latitude, altitude, and ocean currents can affect climate. Climate affects cultures. • A wise use of resources is necessary for a healthy environment.
GOVERNMENT/ CITIZENSHIP	• The U.S. is a democracy in which voters are free to choose their leaders in local, state, and national governments. • Each level of government handles different kinds of problems and functions. • Americans share pride in a heritage they have built together.	• The U.S. is a democracy. • The U.S. Constitution contains the beliefs of the colonists about freedom, equality, justice, and property. • It establishes the branches of the government. • The Constitution (including the Bill of Rights) has been the basis for the rights of Americans.	• Governments vary from dictatorships to democracies. • Ancient Greek and Roman governments influenced our own. • The roles of citizens can vary from no participation to making many political choices. • Economic upheavals and new political ideas can change government.
ECONOMICS	• Americans do many jobs that are created by the U.S.'s wealth, natural and human resources, education, and freedom to make choices as interdependent consumers and producers. • Transportation and communications systems allow the exchange of goods and materials produced in different places.	• Americans have several ways of acquiring goods, services, and property. • Natural resources and technology have influenced economic activities in different U.S. regions. • Changes in transportation and communication have affected economic activities.	• Nations trade with one another to obtain needed raw materials and goods. • Economic development is affected by a nation's government, resources, technology, trade policies, and trade practices.
SOCIOLOGY/ ANTHROPOLOGY	• Individual Americans, though diverse in occupation, family heritage, and other human characteristics, share certain American customs, languages, and symbols.	• American Indians had developed cultures before the arrival of European settlers. • Different groups have made contributions to U.S. society. • American traditions influence our approach to issues such as minority rights and conservation of resources.	• The values and beliefs of a culture influence its growth and development. • The culture of a society includes its customs and religious beliefs. • Advanced cultures have writing, art and architecture, science, and mathematics. • Trade and war can lead to the diffusion of cultures and to new cultures.

SKILLS SCOPE AND SEQUENCE

NUMBERS = PE CHAPTERS

		A	B	C	D	E	F
GEOGRAPHY AND OTHER SOCIAL STUDIES SKILLS	Understanding globes	8	4	8	14		2, 12, 18
	Understanding time zones						1, 17
	Using map keys	7	1, 4, 9	1, 2, 12	1, 4, 6, 8, 10, 12, 13	3, 4, 5, 6, 8, 10, 11, 13, 14, 16, 17	2, 4, 7, 8, 10, 14, 19, 20
	Using scale and distance			1, 2, 12	4, 5, 10, 11, 14	2, 5	6, 9, 15, 16
	Working with directions	6, 7, 8, 9, 10	1, 4, 9, 11	1, 2, 3, 4, 5, 6	1, 4, 6, 7, 8, 10, 12, 13, 15	2, 8, 9	9
	Working with landforms	8	1, 5	2, 5	1, 4, 5, 7, 8, 9, 10, 11, 12	2, 17	2, 12, 16, 17, 18
	Working with latitude and longitude						2, 12, 16
	Working with maps	7, 8, 9	1, 4, 9, 10, 11	1, 2, 3, 4, 5, 6, 10, 11, 12, 13, 14	1, 2, 4, 5, 6, 7, 8, 9, 10, 11, 12, 13, 14	1, 2, 3, 4, 5, 6, 8, 9, 10, 11, 13, 14, 16, 17	1, 2, 3, 4, 5, 6, 7, 8, 9, 10, 11, 12, 13, 14, 15, 16, 17, 18, 19, 20
	Working with graphs	6	5, 7	9, 11	2, 3, 11	11, 12, 14	15, 16
	Working with time lines		12	13	13, 15	2, 5, 6	9
	Working with charts	11	3, 9	9, 11	7	2, 4, 7	6, 10
	Working with diagrams			8, 12, 15	3, 14		
	Working with tables				6		
THEMATIC STRANDS IN SOCIAL STUDIES	Culture	1, 2, 3, 4, 5, 6, 7, 8, 9, 10, 11, 12	1, 3, 4, 5, 6, 7, 8, 9, 10, 11, 12	1, 2, 3, 4, 5, 6, 7, 8, 9, 10, 11, 12, 13, 14, 15, 16	1, 2, 3, 5, 6, 7, 9, 10, 11, 12, 13, 14, 15	1, 2, 3, 4, 5, 6, 7, 8, 9, 10, 11, 12, 13, 14, 15, 16, 17, 18	1, 2, 4, 5, 6, 7, 8, 9, 10, 11, 13, 14, 15, 16, 17, 19, 20
	Time, continuity, and change	1, 4, 6, 7, 9, 10, 11, 12	2, 3, 4, 10	1, 3, 6, 9, 12, 13, 14, 15, 16	2, 3, 5, 7, 8, 9, 10, 11, 13, 14, 15	1, 2, 3, 4, 5, 6, 7, 8, 9, 10, 11, 12, 13, 14, 15, 16, 17, 18	1, 4, 5, 6, 7, 8, 9, 10, 11, 13, 14, 15, 16, 17, 18, 19, 20
	People, places, and environments	1, 2, 3, 4, 5, 6, 7, 8, 9, 10, 11, 12	1, 2, 3, 4, 5, 6, 7, 8, 9, 10, 11	1, 2, 3, 4, 5, 6, 7, 8, 9, 10, 11, 12, 13, 14, 15, 16	1, 2, 3, 5, 6, 7, 8, 9, 10, 11, 12, 13, 14, 15	1, 2, 3, 4, 5, 6, 7, 8, 9, 10, 11, 12, 13, 14, 15, 16, 17, 18	1, 2, 3, 4, 5, 6, 7, 8, 9, 10, 11, 12, 13, 14, 15, 16, 17, 18, 19, 20
	Individual development and identity	1, 2, 3, 6, 7, 8, 9, 10, 11, 12	4, 6, 7, 8, 9, 10, 11, 12	1, 3, 4, 5, 6, 8, 9, 10, 11, 12, 13, 14, 15, 16	2, 3, 4, 7, 9, 11, 13, 14, 15	1, 3, 4, 5, 6, 7, 8, 9, 10, 11, 12, 13, 14, 15, 16, 17, 18	4, 5, 6, 7, 8, 9, 10, 11, 13, 14, 15, 16, 19, 20
	Individuals, groups, and institutions	1, 2, 3, 4, 5, 6, 7, 8, 9, 10, 11, 12	1, 2, 3, 4, 5, 6, 7, 8, 9, 10, 11, 12	1, 3, 4, 6, 7, 9, 10, 11, 12, 13, 14, 15, 16	3, 4, 5, 6, 9, 10, 11, 12, 13, 14, 15	1, 2, 3, 4, 5, 6, 7, 8, 9, 10, 11, 12, 13, 14, 15, 16, 17, 18	1, 4, 5, 6, 7, 8, 9, 10, 11, 13, 14, 15, 16, 17, 19, 20
	Power, authority, and governance	1, 2, 3, 4, 5, 6, 7, 8, 9, 12	6, 7, 8, 9, 10, 11	1, 2, 3, 7, 9, 10, 11, 12, 14, 15, 16	3, 7, 9, 11, 13, 15	3, 4, 5, 6, 7, 8, 9, 10, 11, 12, 13, 14, 15, 16, 17, 18	1, 4, 5, 6, 7, 8, 9, 10, 11, 13, 14, 15, 16, 17, 19, 20
	Production, distribution, and consumption	3, 4, 5, 8, 10, 11	3, 4, 5, 6, 7, 9	1, 3, 5, 7, 8, 12, 13, 14	5, 6, 7, 8, 9, 11, 12, 13, 15	1, 3, 4, 5, 9, 10, 11, 12, 13, 14, 15, 16, 17, 18	1, 3, 4, 5, 6, 7, 8, 10, 11, 12, 13, 14, 15, 16, 17, 19
	Science, technology, and society	1, 4, 5, 7, 9	2, 5, 7, 10	1, 4, 7, 8, 10, 13, 14	1, 7, 9, 13, 14, 15	2, 3, 10, 11, 12, 13, 14, 15, 16, 17, 18	1, 3, 4, 5, 6, 8, 9, 10, 11, 13, 14, 15, 16, 18, 20
	Global connections	2, 3, 6, 8, 9, 12	1, 3, 4, 5, 10, 11, 12	5, 6, 8, 11, 16	2, 4, 5, 6, 7, 8, 10, 12, 14, 15	1, 2, 3, 5, 6, 10, 12, 15, 16, 17, 18	1, 2, 3, 4, 6, 7, 8, 9, 10, 11, 13, 14, 16, 17, 19
	Civic ideals and practice	4, 5, 6, 7, 9, 12	4, 5, 7, 8, 9, 10, 11, 12	1, 3, 7, 8, 9, 10, 11, 12, 13, 14, 15, 16	3, 4, 7, 9, 13	3, 4, 5, 6, 7, 10, 11, 12, 15, 17, 18	3, 4, 5, 6, 8, 9, 10, 11, 15, 16

UNIT 1 — What Is a Community? (pages 5–23)

Unit Summary People live together in communities all over the world. A community is the place where they live, work, and play. People live together in groups because they can help one another and get things done more easily. Life in communities depends in part on natural resources, such as water, forests, soil, and mineral wealth. Community life also is affected by climate and area landforms.

Before Reading the Unit Write the word *community* on the chalkboard and ask students to tell you what it means. List their definitions under the word. Then call on a volunteer to look up the word in a dictionary and share the definition with the class. Next, extend the discussion by asking students to read the unit opener on page 5 and discuss the photograph. What can students tell about the community by looking at the photo? Show students the Unit Project box. Explain that they will work on this project throughout the unit.

Unit Project

Setting Up the Project Students will find that their bulletin board displays will be more interesting and exciting if they collect a wide variety of facts and visual material. Suggest various sources for information available in the community, such as the school and public library.

Suggest that students set up folders to organize the material they find. They might want to set up folders by subject—businesses, landforms, maps, and so on—so they can easily choose the best material in each category for their display.

Point out to students that the Project Tips in each chapter offer specific suggestions for moving the project along. Urge students to adapt the suggestions to their own interests.

Presenting the Project One alternative presentation possibility might be to create a young person's guide to the community. The class could divide the work according to their interests and talents. Some students could write material about special places, important landforms, and how weather affects life in the community; others could draw illustrations and design the book. The chamber of commerce and school or local newspapers might want to publish students' work.

After Reading the Unit Encourage discussion of the unit opener questions. Prompt students by asking questions, such as: Why is it beneficial for people to live in communities? How are communities affected by land, natural resources, and climate?

Skill Builder
Using a Landform Map
As students begin work on page 22, remind them to study the map key. Make sure all the students understand that the symbols used on the map are explained in the key. Review this concept by pointing out the symbol for a city in the key and having students find it on the map.

Answers: 1. mountains and plains **2.** Students should correctly identify plains and mountains. **3.** Little Rock **4.** It is flat; it is made up of plains.

Teacher's Resource Binder

Blackline Masters for Unit 1: Unit 1 Project Organizer, Unit 1 Review, Unit 1 Test; Activities for Chapters 1, 2; Outline Map of the United States

CHAPTER 1 / People and Places (pages 6–13)

Chapter Summary People live in communities so they can help one another and accomplish things no individual can accomplish alone. In any community, individuals depend on the jobs done by others and on businesses run by others. The businesses, in turn, depend on members of the community. As a community, people also share many public places, such as libraries and parks. Capitals are communities that serve as the seat of government.

Chapter Objectives Students will learn to

- explain why people live in communities.
- explain what a state capital is.
- use a map key and read symbols on a map.
- identify and use a compass rose.
- identify and use the distance scale on a map.
- state an example of how people and communities depend on one another.
- list examples of businesses and public places in a community.

Vocabulary	
community, p. 6	distance scale, p. 8
capital, p. 7	depend on, p. 9
symbols, p. 7	businesses, p. 10
map key, p. 7	public, p. 11
compass rose, p. 7	

Vocabulary Activities Read aloud the etymology of the word *capital:* The word *capital* comes from the Latin word *caput,* which means *head.* Explain that a capital city is the head of a state, because it is the place where the state government meets. Ask students which kind of letter is used for the head, or beginning, of a sentence (capital). For students who have difficulty with any of the vocabulary terms, help them use the glossary to find the meanings of the terms.

Before Reading the Chapter Ask students to discuss what it means to depend on someone or something. Ask them to give an example of something they count on, such as the time the school bus comes or the time school ends every day. Ask students why it is important to depend on people and events.

Teaching Suggestions and Answers

Page 6
After reading the first paragraph, ask students to name their own community. On the chalkboard, help students make a list of places in their community where people live, work, and play. **Students should answer that people in communities can help each other and more easily get things done.**

Page 7
Ask students to locate New Mexico on a map of the United States. Then have them locate Santa Fe on the map. **Students should answer that the symbol stands for the state capital. They should circle the star symbol and Santa Fe on the map; circle the symbol for interstate highway; circle the compass rose and answer north.**

Page 8
Remind students that maps are drawings of real places. Work with students to make sure they understand how to use a distance scale. To provide students with extra practice using a distance scale, have them find the distance between the Capitol Complex and the Museum of Indian Arts and Culture (one and one-quarter miles). Point out to students that they can also use the distance scale to find distances in kilometers. **Students should find that the distance from the cathedral to the museum is about one and one-half miles.**

Page 9
Have students look at the photograph at the top of the page. Draw their attention to the adobe-style buildings in the background. Explain that the city was founded by Spanish people in the 1600s. The nearby Pueblo Indians built homes of adobe, a mixture of earth, straw, and water. The Spanish did the same, making their homes and other buildings of adobe bricks. One adobe

building in Santa Fe was built in 1610. It has often been repaired and is still used. **Students may answer that people do not want their community to look like any other, that they want it to stand out.**

Page 10

Ask students to make a list of the kinds of stores in their community. **Students should identify picture 1 as a gas station, picture 2 as a supermarket, and picture 3 as a clothing store.**

Page 11

Discuss with students the differences between private and public property. Help students understand that public places belong to everyone in a community and that everyone must help take care of them. **Students should circle the card catalog.**

Project Tip

Help students carry out the suggestion on page 11. Students may need special help in thinking about public places to include. Remind them that public places include city hall, schools, city parks, swimming pools, and beaches, libraries, and museums.

Page 12

Special People Tell students that when Jacob Lawrence was a teenager, he loved art so much that he would walk 50 blocks from his neighborhood to the Metropolitan Museum of Art, a major museum in New York City. You might ask students what they like about art and urge them to paint pictures of their community. **Students should circle the numbers the girls are writing on the chalkboard.**

Page 13

Chapter Checkup You may want to work through the Chapter Checkup with students. Make sure they all understand what the correct answers are to the numbered questions.

Answers: 1. b 2. b 3. d 4. a 5. c 6. d
Have several students volunteer their ideas. They may give many specific examples of interdependency. For instance, students may say they need things from stores, and that stores need their business.

After Reading the Chapter

Have students make a class list of reasons why people need communities. You might also make a list of public places in your community that the class could visit.

Social Studies

Suggest that students interview people in their neighborhood about the jobs they do in the community.

Writing

Have students note the condition of roads, playgrounds, or other facilities in their community. If any of them need repair, have students write a class letter to alert the appropriate local officials to the situation.

Art

Have students create drawings of their community. Tell students to include in the drawings pictures of places where people work, live, and play. Encourage students to show people engaged in work or play in their drawings.

Writing

Have students interview someone who works in a public place such as a library, school, community park or beach, or museum. Have students find out what the person does for the community. Ask students to write a paragraph describing what the person does and how the job she or he does helps the community.

CHAPTER 2 / Communities and Their Geography (pages 14–21)

Chapter Summary The natural resources, climate, and landforms of a community are part of its geography. Natural resources include water, soil, forests, sea life, and minerals. Weather and climate can affect the economies of communities. Nearby landforms influence the development of a community and affect human settlement and work.

Chapter Objectives Students will learn to

- explain how landforms, weather, and climate affect communities.
- identify a place in the community where water exists.
- identify examples of natural resources.
- identify how climate can help a community.
- read a landform map.
- explain how landforms affect communities.

Vocabulary	
weather, p. 14	landforms, p. 18
natural resource, p. 15	plains, p. 18
	mountains, p. 18
minerals, p. 16	valley, p. 19
climate, p. 17	canyon, p. 19

Vocabulary Activities Work with students to build a word web to identify natural resources. You may use the Concept Web found on page 63 of this guide for this activity. Write *natural resources* at the center of the web. As students read the chapter, have them add examples of natural resources to the web. Once the web is completed, ask students to draw a picture showing how people depend on natural resources.

Before Reading the Chapter Make sure students understand the term *geography*. Ask students to define the word, and write their definitions on the chalkboard. If most of the definitions concern the natural world, point out that geography also studies the world of communities. You may want to complete the discussion by writing the following definition on the chalkboard: Geography is the study of Earth and how we live on it.

Teaching Suggestions and Answers

Page 14

If you have a wall map, ask students to locate Chicago and Lake Michigan. Then help students to find other important cities in the United States that are located near water. **Students should draw an arrow to one of the skyscrapers shown in the photograph. Answers may include an ocean, a bay, a gulf, a river, a lake, or a pond.**

Page 15

Discuss the natural resources your community has, including the different kinds of plants and trees found in your community. You might also ask students to name building materials other than wood that might be used to build homes. Ask students if most of the buildings in Santa Fe are made of wood (no). **Answers may include water, trees, or good soil.**

Page 16

Help students make a list of minerals other than those mentioned in the text. These might include iron, lead, coal, copper, or even diamonds. Then ask students to list items that are powered by gas and oil. Tell students that scientists who study minerals say that everything we have in our world comes from the ground, and if these things cannot be grown, they have to be mined. Conclude with a short discussion on the reasons people need to conserve natural resources. **Students should circle the fisherman's net. They should put an X at the bottom of the oil drill and circle the car and the truck.**

Page 17

Discuss how climate affects people's lives. Ask students how they were affected by today's weather. Ask why climate is important when people plan a vacation. Then have students locate Honolulu, Hawaii, Colorado, and Utah on a map of the United States. **Students should circle the sand, water, trees, or air in the picture of Honolulu. They should answer that both sunny, warm weather and snow can help a community.**

Page 18

Ask students if they have ever pedaled a bicycle up a hill. Have them explain how it was different from riding on flat land. Then ask students if they live in an area of mountains or plains. If neither, encourage them to describe the land. Then ask them how the shape of the land affects their community. Point out that the map of North Carolina on this page shows not only the state, but also the shape of the land and some products the state produces. You might want to help students use the key to identify some of North Carolina's agricultural products. Ask: What is grown near Charlotte? Help students use the key to identify soybeans as the main crop grown near Charlotte. **Students should put a checkmark in front of the Appalachian Mountains and the Blue Ridge Mountains and write the answer** *plains*.

Page 19

Explain that the Navajo land covers 17 million acres of the southwestern United States in the states of Arizona, Utah, and New Mexico. It is a land of vividly colored canyons, rugged mountains, and areas of dry, flat land. Have students find this area on a map and compare it with the land around their community. Ask students to discuss why it is hard to farm on mountainsides. **Answers may include mountains, plains, valleys, hills, or canyons. Students should circle the cable car in the photograph.**

Project Tip

You may want to suggest that students research a landform map of the state in an encyclopedia or book about the state. These references also should include information on weather and climate in the community.

Page 20

Around the Globe Help students locate Australia on the map. Point out that Australia is both a continent and a country. Then ask students if they have ever seen a koala in a zoo. Explain that koalas belong to a group of animals whose young grow in a pouch, or pocket, outside the body. Kangaroos belong to this group, too. **Students should answer that Australia is about 7,500 miles southwest of the United States. They should circle Brisbane on the east coast of Australia.**

Page 21

Chapter Checkup Work through the Chapter Checkup with students and make sure they all understand what the correct answers are to the numbered questions.

Answers: 1. b **2.** d **3.** a **4.** d **5.** c **6.** b

Students might say that it is easier to build structures and roads and to move around on flat land. It is harder to move materials up a mountainside to build houses. It is harder to farm in the mountains because they are rough and steep, and generally the soil is less fertile and more rocky.

After Reading the Chapter

Have students work together in small groups to make a picture chart showing the many uses of water. Display it in the classroom with captions explaining each use.

Science

Ask students to keep weather diaries for a week. They should note the number of hours of sun and rain and the temperature range for each day. Ask students to consider how the weather they observed affects local businesses.

Writing

You might ask students to write a short description of their favorite landform. Urge them to use sensory words that describe its color and shape. Tell them to explain what it is like to walk across this kind of land.

Art

Help students gain a better understanding of the importance of water as a natural resource. Ask them to work in small groups to make a poster showing the many ways people use water.

UNIT 2 Kinds of Communities (pages 24–51)

Unit Summary Communities are called towns, suburbs, or cities depending on their size and other characteristics. Rural communities are usually small farming or fishing towns. Many medium-sized communities are suburbs located near big cities. Cities are bigger and noisier than towns and suburbs.

Before Reading the Unit Encourage students to discuss what they know about different-sized communities. Ask them to describe the smallest and the biggest communities they have ever seen, heard about, or lived in. What is life like in these different communities? What work do people do? Extend the discussion to find out what students want to learn about different kinds of communities. Ask a volunteer to read aloud the unit opener on page 24. Then discuss the photograph as a class, keeping the unit opener questions in mind. Ask students to imagine they can step into the photograph and explore the town. What would they like to do? What do they find most interesting? Is the town different from their community? If so, how? Encourage students to keep the unit opener questions in mind as they read the unit. Remind them that they will find answers to these questions and others as they study Unit 2.

Point out the Unit Project box and explain that students will work on this project as they study Unit 2.

Unit Project

Setting Up the Project To stimulate students' imaginations, bring a variety of travel brochures to class. Have students meet in teams, and give each group a variety of brochures to study as models. Remind students that their brochures should help visitors feel at home in the community. Explain what visitors would want to know about the community. Tell students to look for pictures of towns, suburbs, and cities in newspapers and in travel and home magazines. Students can make postcards by drawing pictures or clipping photographs and gluing them to 4- by 6-inch index cards.

Remind students that the Project Tips in each chapter can help spark their imaginations.

Presenting the Project One additional possibility might be for students to "mail" the postcards they make to one another, to another class, or to friends who live in other communities. Students should write as if they lived in the town, suburb, or city they have created. They should tell their distant friends what life is like where they live.

After Reading the Unit Ask students: What are some ways communities are different from one another? How do community populations differ? How do jobs in communities differ? How do ways of life differ? What kind of community do you live in?

Skill Builder
Reading a Political Map
Before students read page 50, review the meaning of the word *border* with them. Be sure that they understand that a border is the point at which one place, such as a state, ends, and another begins.

Answers: 1. Students should circle the river symbol in the map key. **2.** Students should trace the path of the Yukon River. **3.** Students should circle Juneau. **4.** Arctic Ocean **5.** Canada

Teacher's Resource Binder
Blackline Masters for Unit 2: Unit 2 Project Organizer, Unit 2 Review, Unit 2 Test; Activities for Chapters 3, 4, 5, 6; Outline Map of the United States

CHAPTER 3 / Small Communities (pages 25–30)

Chapter Summary People enjoy quiet and friendliness in small communities. They use the same businesses, work at similar kinds of jobs, and see one another frequently. Small towns are often rural, with small populations; as a result, they depend on volunteers for many city services.

Chapter Objectives Students will learn to

- explain why people in small communities get to know one another easily.
- identify some jobs and land uses common to small communities.
- explain why volunteers are important to small communities.

Vocabulary	
docks, p. 25	population, p. 27
rural, p. 27	volunteer, p. 28

Vocabulary Activities To help students understand the word *rural*, have them make a collage of pictures showing rural scenes. They can cut pictures from old magazines or draw their own. Mount the pictures on a large sheet of paper and display them in the classroom under the title "Rural." If students have problems with any of the vocabulary words, help them use the glossary.

Before Reading the Chapter Ask students if any of them have lived in small communities. Encourage them to describe the experience for the class. What did they like about living there? Write their comments on the chalkboard. Then ask for volunteers who have lived in large communities and repeat the exercise. Have the class compare the two lists.

Teaching Suggestions and Answers
Page 25
Tell students that they could think of their grade in school as a small community. Ask them to list ways in which their grade is like a small town. They should recognize that they make up a small number of people who see each other often and who do the same kind of work. **Students should circle a dock in the photograph.**

Page 26
Point out that people who live on the same block or in the same neighborhood of a large community are often friendly, too. Sometimes, people say that big cities are really a collection of neighborhoods, or small towns. Many neighborhoods in large cities have their own names and identities. If possible, show students a neighborhood map of New York City, Chicago, or San Francisco. Name some of the different neighborhoods for students and point them out on the map. You might have students role-play what to say when they meet someone in public. **Students should put a checkmark on the store in the photograph. They should circle the pet food dish that the woman is carrying in the plastic bag. They should put an *X* on the truck in the picture.**

Page 27
Have students locate Rose Hill, North Carolina, on the map on page 18. Ask students what the land looks like around Rose Hill. Inform students that the population of Rose Hill (in the 2000 Census) was 1,330. Then ask students to compare the population of Rose Hill to the population of their community. Help students understand that jobs in rural areas and small towns are not limited to farming. Explain that even the smallest towns have gas stations, stores or shops, and restaurants where people work. **Students should circle what the Langs have grown. They should answer that there is not enough space in the city.**

Page 28
Ask students to name other kinds of volunteer work. Remind them that people often volunteer to help in hospitals and to raise money to benefit communities. Discuss the kind of fire department and garbage removal service in your community. Make sure students understand how important both of these services are for the community's safety and health. **Students should answer that it is cheaper for a community to use volunteers.**

Project Tip
Help students carry out the suggestion on page 28. Suggest that students look for pictures that show many aspects of life in small towns. They should look for pictures of people at work on farms and in stores, offices, and fire departments. They should also look for pictures of people having fun. Discarded travel magazines will be rich sources. Urge them to find as many pictures as they can of small towns in different parts of the country. Students may find books filled with photographs of small towns in the library. They can use the photographs as models for their own drawings.

Page 29
For Your Information Have students locate Florida, Connecticut, Idaho, Pennsylvania, and Montana on a map of the United States. Then give students a map of your state and have them find more communities with unusual names. Have the class vote on its favorite unusual name. **Students should circle Sugar Land in Texas, Paw Paw in Michigan, and Winter in Wisconsin. Students should write the names of any other two communities shown on the map.**

Page 30
Chapter Checkup Help students work through the Chapter Checkup. Make sure all students understand what the correct answers are to the numbered questions.

Answers: 1. d **2.** c **3.** a **4.** d **5.** c **6.** b
Students will probably focus on having many friends. You may want to have students volunteer some of their thoughts. Discuss the pace of life in a small town. Is it slower than life in a big community?

After Reading the Chapter
Ask students to discuss ways of being friendly. How do they show friendliness? What do they say and do? How does this make others feel? Then ask them why it is harder for people in very large communities to be friendly all the time.

Art
Students can paint a class mural that depicts the main street of a small town. Before students begin painting, suggest that they decide what the main business in town will be and what buildings should be included.

Writing
Have students write a short story about the Lang family. Invite them to study the picture on page 27. Then have them tell a story about what the Langs are going to do when they finish packing the vegetables. Tell them to use things they learned about small towns in their story.

Social Studies
If possible, arrange a field trip for students to visit a farm. Have students prepare a list of questions beforehand to ask while they are at the farm. For example, students should find out what kinds of crops are grown or what kind of livestock is raised. Encourage students also to find out why certain crops or livestock are raised in your region.

Drama
Invite small groups of students to perform a short play about the people in a small town. Students may want to make the setting of the play be a farm.

Geography
Point out to students that many communities get their names from the kinds of landforms that are nearby. Have students work in small groups. Provide each group with a different state map that shows physical features such as rivers, lakes, and mountains. (State maps from a road atlas would work well for this activity.) Challenge students to make a list of interesting community names that relate to the physical features near the town.

CHAPTER 4 / Suburban Communities (pages 31–36)

Chapter Summary Many people choose to live in suburbs because suburbs are quiet and friendly like small towns, yet close to city jobs and activities. Good transportation is a key part of suburban life. People in suburbs drive to work, shopping, and activities, and many take subways into the nearby city.

Chapter Objectives Students will learn to

- describe a suburb.
- explain why some people choose to live in suburbs.
- name the kinds of transportation people use to get around suburbs and to travel to and from cities.
- use a compass rose to identify an intermediate direction on a map.

Vocabulary	
suburbs, p. 31	transportation, p. 33

Vocabulary Activities Draw a chart with these headings on a large sheet of graph paper: *Land/Air/Water.* Then ask students to name as many kinds of transportation as they can for each heading. (Possible answers include: Land: car, bus, truck, bike, motorcycle, train, subway, van, skateboard, roller skates; Air: jet, helicopter, blimp, hot-air balloon, airplane, hang glider; Water: canoe, rowboat, ocean liner, raft, ferry, yacht, sailboat.) You might ask students to illustrate types of transportation listed on the chart. Remind students to use the glossary to find the meanings of words they find difficult.

Before Reading the Chapter Discuss how people in your community get to work, school, stores, and other places. Compare the different means of transportation. Which is quickest? Easiest? Safest? Cheapest?

Teaching Suggestions and Answers

Page 31
Ask students to locate Atlanta, Georgia, on a map of the United States. Point out that Atlanta is the capital of Georgia. You might also tell students that Atlanta's first suburb was Inman Park. It was built over 100 years ago and is full of historic houses today. **Students should answer that many houses are grouped close together like neighborhoods in a city.**

Page 32
Survey the class to find out how many students have family members who work in another community. Also ask students how they get to school. You might want to make a chart on the chalkboard to show the different kinds of transportation students use to get to school. **Answers may include: room for a garden; the suburb feels like a small town; the streets are quiet.**

Page 33
Be sure students understand that transportation is not limited to motor- or engine-powered vehicles. Any means of moving from one place to another is a form of transportation. Inform students that in many countries the bicycle is a very important form of transportation. In China, for example, people use bicycles to get to work and to transport goods. Point out that suburbs grew quickly in the United States once many people were able to own cars. By 1976 most Americans lived in suburbs. Explain that cars have helped make suburbs look the way they do. As an example, invite students to describe a typical shopping center or mall. How is it built for people who travel by car? **Students should circle a car, truck, or other vehicle shown in the photograph of the expressway.**

Project Tip
Tell students that a librarian at their school or public library may help them find facts about suburbs and the people who live in them. Students may have difficulty finding pictures that distinguish suburbs from small towns. Tell them to look for photographs or draw pictures that include a small downtown, a subway or train station, houses with lawns and shade trees and cars in the driveway. They might find photographs or draw pictures of commuters waiting for a train. Another possibility might be pictures or photographs of people at a suburban shopping mall.

Page 34

Explain that cars are a form of private transportation. Point out that the commuter trains in San Francisco are a form of public transportation. Ask students what *public* means. Who can use these trains? Talk about some of the benefits of using public transportation, including saving money and reducing pollution. Review the answers students offer to be sure they understand how to read intermediate directions. If students need extra practice with intermediate directions, ask them to name the community that is directly southeast of Redwood City (Menlo Park) and the community that is directly northeast of Pacifica (Daly City). **Students should draw a line from San Francisco to Union City. They should draw a line under one of the following communities located southwest of Union City: Redwood City, Menlo Park, Palo Alto, Mountain View. They should put a checkmark in front of one of these communities located northwest of Union City: San Francisco, Oakland, Berkeley, Daly City, Pacifica, Hayward, Castro Valley.**

Page 35

Technology Tell students that BART stands for Bay Area Rapid Transit. Point out that many cities in the United States have subway systems. These include Atlanta, New York City, Washington, D.C., Chicago, Baltimore, and Philadelphia. **Answers may include: subways are faster than cars because they don't get caught in traffic and they don't have to park; subways are cheaper; some people don't have cars.**

Page 36

Chapter Checkup You may want to make sure all students understand what the correct answers are to the numbered questions by working through the Chapter Checkup with the students.

Answers: 1. b **2.** a **3.** c **4.** b **5.** d **6.** d
Many students might say that people who live in suburbs can enjoy a sort of small-town life but still work in the city; also, they can go to nearby shopping centers.

After Reading the Chapter

Ask students to think of some of their favorite television programs. Which ones take place in the suburbs? Discuss the reasons for students' choices.

Writing
Have students describe a set for a television show that takes place in the suburbs. Tell them to use vivid details.

Art/City Planning
Have students work in groups to design and draw a picture map of a suburb. Have them give the suburb a name. Direct students to include private residences as well as public places such as schools, parks, community centers, train and/or bus stations, and so on. Have students label the buildings and other features on their picture map.

Social Studies
Have interested students investigate some of the more unusual forms of transportation. For instance, students may want to find out about zeppelins, hydrofoils, high-speed "bullet" trains, or trolleys. Have students explain the special uses and advantages of such kinds of transportation.

CHAPTER 5 / Cities

(pages 37–42)

Chapter Summary Cities are the largest of all communities. Because of the large numbers of people living on a limited amount of land, many people live in apartments, major businesses are clustered downtown, and the city must rely on ships, trains, and planes for shipments of food and other goods. Cities offer a wide variety of job possibilities, including work in factories, as well as diverse recreational outlets.

Chapter Objectives Students will learn to

- describe cities and name sections in cities, such as the downtown area.
- list some jobs that people in cities do.
- explain what factories produce.
- list some things that cities provide for fun.

Vocabulary	
harbor, p. 38	goods, p. 39
factories, p. 39	

Vocabulary Activities Have students write an acrostic poem using the word *factories*. Write the word vertically on the board. Explain that each line of the poem must begin with a letter in *factories*. The first word in the first line will begin with *F*. You might point out that this kind of poem does not have to rhyme. Each line should describe workers in a factory or name goods that are made in factories. Help students use the glossary if they have difficulty with any of the terms.

Before Reading the Chapter Invite students to describe visits they have made to special places in big cities, such as museums, sports arenas, zoos, parks, or shopping areas. Ask students to describe what most impressed them about the experience. For students who do not live in cities, ask them to explain how these places compared with places in their community.

Teaching Suggestions and Answers

Page 37
Have students find Los Angeles, California, on a map of the United States. Then ask students to compare the population of Los Angeles (nearly 4 million in 2000) with the population of your community. **Students should place a checkmark on skyscrapers or sprawling neighborhoods.**

Page 38
Make sure that all students know what a harbor is. Then discuss why a harbor is often surrounded by warehouses. Ask students to suggest ways that goods might be transported to and from communities that do not have harbors. Tell students that many of the large cities in the United States became large cities because they had harbors and most trade relied on ship travel before the 1800s. You might want to tell students that cities with large harbors are often called port cities. Show students where Boston, Massachusetts, is on a map. Explain that Boston, with a harbor on the Atlantic Ocean, was one of our country's first cities. Important businesses in Boston were fishing, shipbuilding, and trade between the United States and Europe. **Students should put an X on the harbor. Students should answer that you would travel northeast from the stores on Park Lane to the bridge. Students should trace a route east on Water Street to Bruce Street and then north to the apartments.**

Page 39
Point out that some cities are centers for certain kinds of industries, such as publishing, manufacturing, and entertainment. Then ask students to think about the kinds of goods they use that are made in factories. Work with students to make a list of manufactured goods. **Students should circle the car in the photograph.**

Page 40
Ask students to locate Austin, Texas, on a map of the United States. Explain that Austin, like all big cities, has a variety of things to do. Point out that some other things to do in big cities include visiting galleries that show works of art, eating in restaurants that serve foods from many parts of the world, touring historic buildings, viewing the city from the tops of skyscrapers, and visiting museums with everything from puppets to lasers. **Student answers will vary.**

19

Project Tip
Urge students to look for a variety of pictures, from cityscapes that show skylines and general views of diverse areas to closeups of people, jobs, and activities. Encourage students to find night shots, too, since cities are busy around the clock.

Page 41
Around the Globe Ask students to locate Toronto, Ontario, and Canada on a map of North America. Point out that Toronto is Canada's largest city. Direct students' attention to the photograph. Tell students that this is a photo of Toronto's City Hall, which was completed in 1965. The saucer-shaped part of the building is where the city's leaders meet. **Toronto is like some big cities in the United States because it is a big transportation center. Also, many people in Toronto work in factories.**

Page 42
Chapter Checkup You may want to work through the Chapter Checkup with students. Make sure they all understand what the correct answers are to the numbered questions.

Answers: 1. d **2.** a **3.** c **4.** d **5.** c **6.** b
Students' answers may include the fact that the city is big, with millions of people; it has glass skyscrapers where people live, work, and shop; people work at many interesting jobs; they can see plays and sports and hear live music.

After Reading the Chapter
To remind students that space is a precious commodity in cities, have them make a large cutaway picture of a skyscraper. They might show stores on the lower floors and offices and apartments on the upper floors. Students may enjoy making up stories about the various scenes in the buildings they create.

Social Studies
Take a walk through the Yellow Pages. Bring a copy of the Yellow Pages for your community to class. Encourage students to note how many different kinds of businesses operate in your community.

Writing
Read aloud a few poems about city life. Possible titles include: "Just for One Day," by Lillian Morrison; "Sing a Song of Subways," by Eve Merriam; and "The People Upstairs," by Ogden Nash. Then ask students to write a city poem using what they've learned from the chapter and from their own experiences.

Art
Have small groups of students design and draw a mural of a modern or futuristic cityscape. To provide inspiration, you might make available some books or magazines with pictures of modern skyscrapers.

History
Gather some information and pictures about ancient cities such as those of Mesopotamia (Ur), Latin America (Tenochtitlán), or ancient Egypt (Memphis, Thebes, or Akhetaton). Be sure students understand that many different types of cities have existed throughout history. Alternately, you could show students pictures and photos of historical European cities such as Rome and Athens. Discuss with students the similarities and differences between modern and ancient cities.

Science and Industry
If you live in or near a city, you may be able to arrange for your class to tour a factory or manufacturing facility. After the tour, have students write a paragraph about what they found most interesting about the manufacturing process.

Making a Chart
Help students use an almanac and other reference books to find the ten largest cities in the United States. Then have students work in small groups to make a chart of the information they located. Headings for the chart could include the name of the state where the city is located and the name of the state capital as well as the names of the ten cities and their populations.

CHAPTER 6 / Your Own Community (pages 43–49)

Chapter Summary A community can be a small town, a suburb, or a city. Every community has a unique history and unique characteristics.

Chapter Objectives Students will learn to

- compare small towns, suburbs, and cities.
- identify the kind of community in which they live.
- write their names and addresses.
- read a political map.
- identify their state on a U.S. map.
- research information about their community.
- compare a community of the past with a contemporary one.

Vocabulary	
address, p. 44	borders, p. 44
political map, p. 44	slaves, p. 48

Vocabulary Activities Write a sentence on the chalkboard that includes the word *address*. Use the word *address* to start a discussion on the importance of knowing your address and writing it correctly. Ask students what might happen if you incorrectly filled in your address on a form. Ask what might happen if you wrote the wrong address on a letter you were sending. Ask students why people keep books with addresses in them. If students have problems with any of the vocabulary terms, help them use the glossary.

Before Reading the Chapter Point out to students that every community's history shapes the community we know today. Ask volunteers to tell the class any facts they know about their community's past. Then tell students they are going to explore the things that make their community special. Introduce students to resource books and other materials they might use while researching their community. At this point, you might want to tour the school or public library with the class.

Teaching Suggestions and Answers

Page 43
Ask students to explain how goods that arrive by ship in Harbor City might get to Cornhusk. **Students should put a checkmark under Harbor City. They should put an *X* under Cornhusk. They should draw a line under Westville. Students should circle the drawing that shows a community most like their community.**

Page 44
Draw students' attention to the insets of Hawaii and Alaska on the map of the United States. On a globe or a large map show students the true locations of Hawaii and Alaska. Explain that these two states are shown in insets because they are very far away from the other 48 states. Explain to students that they should write their names on the first line, their street address on the second line, and their city and state on the third line. Remind students to include their zip codes with their addresses. Discuss the importance of addresses in linking communities. **Students should write their correct addresses on the lines. They should circle the state they live in. Students should identify one of the following states as a state that borders Mexico: California, Arizona, New Mexico, or Texas.**

Page 45
Ask volunteers to share the questions they make up. List the questions on the chalkboard and encourage students to use them in their project research. You might also want to display a large map of your community for students to study. **Student questions will vary.**

Page 46
If possible, ask parents who work in your community to come to class and talk with the students about their jobs. Before students begin their research, discuss ways they can present the information they find. Some possibilities include: a tourist guide listing interesting places to visit or a "resource map" showing crops or livestock raised in your community or state (refer students to the map of North Carolina on page 18).

21

If you live in a fairly large city, students may be able to access useful information about your community by using the Internet. **Student questions will vary.**

Page 47

Ask students to study the photograph and read the caption. Explain to students that many new settlers wanted to come to Skagway after they heard gold had been discovered. In 1898, a railroad was built between White Horse in Canada's Yukon Territory and Skagway. Ask students whether they think the population of Skagway increased or decreased after the completion of the railroad (improved transportation to the area would have caused the population to increase). Explain to students that photographs can tell us things about the past that are not often found in history books. They tell us about everyday life, the clothes people wore, their hairstyles, and the way communities looked. Point out that photographs have only been around for about 170 years. **Students should circle a horse-drawn carriage or wagon. They may say they know the photograph is old because of the clothing people are wearing, the way the shops and the streets look, and the kind of transportation being used.**

Project Tip

After students read the Project Tip, you might suggest that students write these questions and the questions the class developed in their research notebooks. Remind students that questions will arise as they do research. They should add these questions to their lists and try to answer them.

Page 48

Special People Tell students that Phillis Wheatley learned to speak English within sixteen months after she arrived from Africa. Explain that, like most writers, Phillis chose subjects that she felt strongly about. Urge students to recall things that have given them strong feelings. Anything that touched them can be a subject for a poem: a sad or funny experience, a basketball game, a wind storm, caves, skyscrapers or other interesting places, people, sounds, even foods. **Student answers will vary.**

Page 49

Chapter Checkup Make sure all the students understand the correct answers to the numbered questions by working through the Chapter Checkup with the students.

Answers: 1. c **2.** b **3.** a **4.** b **5.** d **6.** b
Answers will vary, but students should focus on the differences in population, location, and the variety of jobs, activities, and places to live and shop.

After Reading the Chapter

Ask students who have grandparents or elderly friends in the community to interview them about their community in the past. Help students put together a list of questions. Suggestions: How long have you lived in your house? Has the block changed much since you've lived here? Are there any buildings you watched being built? What was there before the new building? How has the community changed over the years?

Language Arts

Have students write short fictional stories set in your community's past. Encourage them to use facts about their community to make the setting and story believable.

Writing

Ask students to choose the kind of community they like best. Suggest that they write a poem about life in the community they chose. Explain that the poem does not have to rhyme, but that it should capture some aspect of life in their favorite community.

UNIT 3 — People Work in Communities (pages 52–69)

Unit Summary People in communities work to meet their needs and wants. As workers, people produce goods or provide services; as buyers, they are consumers. Most American workers today hold service jobs. Not all goods are made in one community. One product may be made through the efforts of people in many different communities.

Before Reading the Unit Ask students what they would like to learn about the people and why they work. Ask them to read the unit opener on page 52 and discuss the photograph. Then have students read the questions in the unit opener. Point out that they will learn the answers to these questions and others as they study Unit 3.

Draw students' attention to the Unit Project box. Tell them to keep their project in mind as they work through this unit, jotting down any ideas that come to mind.

Unit Project

Setting Up the Project To help students create effective flow charts, urge them to list fairly simple things that they buy. Tell them they will be making some drawings of the way these goods are made, and that the drawings will be easier if the objects are simple. Explain that a bicycle might be too difficult, but that a gallon of milk, a T-shirt, or a box of pencils will work well.

Students will find specific suggestions in the Project Tip sections of the chapters. Encourage them to adapt the suggestions to their own interests, as long as they are relevant to chapter topics.

Presenting the Project One alternative possibility might be to ask students to do a skit. Team members could assume the roles of workers in their flow chart and explain the steps needed to make their product. Each team member would explain his or her step, then give the floor to the next person.

After Reading the Unit Invite discussion of the unit opener questions. You can prompt discussion by using the following: Give an example of why workers are important to a community. Why does it take many communities to meet our needs and wants? How do communities around the globe help one another?

Skill Builder

Using a Flow Chart
Before students read page 68, you might want to review the vocabulary words *producer, consumer, service, wants,* and *needs*.

Answers: 1. Students should circle the hair stylist. **2.** Students should underline the boy eating an ear of corn. **3.** The woman who had her hair styled. **4.** A want. She didn't need a new hair style to live.

Teacher's Resource Binder

Blackline Masters for Unit 3: Unit 3 Project Organizer, Unit 3 Review, Unit 3 Test; Activities for Chapters 7 and 8; Outline Maps of the United States, the World, and the Globe

CHAPTER 7 / Meeting Needs and Wants (pages 53–60)

Chapter Summary Every person has basic needs for food, clothing, and shelter. But people also have wants, or desires, for things that are not necessary for life. Workers in communities meet these wants and needs. Producers grow or make things for sale. Service workers provide other needs or wants. Consumers buy things they need and want with money they earn from jobs. In the past, most people worked on farms. Today, most people work in service industries.

Chapter Objectives Students will learn to

- distinguish between needs and wants.
- identify producers and consumers.
- explain why community services are important.
- identify examples of community services.

Vocabulary	
shelter, p. 53	producer, p. 54
needs, p. 53	consumer, p. 54
wants, p. 53	service, p. 55

Vocabulary Activities Draw the outline of a large shopping cart on the chalkboard. Write the title *Consumer's Cart* over the picture. Tell students they are consumers who will fill up the cart with things they need and want. Invite volunteers to come to the board and draw a picture or write the name of an item inside the cart that they would like to buy. After each volunteer adds something to the cart, ask the class if the item satisfies a need or a want. After every volunteer has had a chance at the chalkboard, ask students to tell you what a consumer is. Advise students to use the glossary if they have difficulty with any of the terms.

Before Reading the Chapter Hold up a dollar bill and ask students to tell you what it is used for. (People use money to buy things.) Then ask students how people get the money they need to buy things. Briefly talk about the variety of jobs people can do to earn money.

Teaching Suggestions and Answers
Page 53
Ask students to describe different kinds of shelter people use in the United States. (Students might mention houses, townhouses, apartments, trailer homes, houseboats, cabins, motels or hotels.) **Students should write *want* on the line.**

Page 54
Point out that people often need tools and equipment to produce goods. When a producer buys tools needed to produce goods, that producer is also a consumer. **Students should circle the paintbrush the boy is using in the first picture. They should write *producer* below the second picture and write *consumer* below the third picture.**

Project Tip
Help students carry out the suggestion on page 54. Tell students they can develop their lists by brainstorming as a group or by writing individual lists and then sharing them in team discussion.

Page 55
On the chalkboard make a chart with the headings *Services* and *Goods*. Ask students to name examples and list them under each heading. Point out that people can buy services just as they buy goods, using the money they earn. **Students should circle the doctor in the photograph.**

Page 56
Discuss with students why adding chemicals to the water keeps the water purer than adding nothing at all. Then ask students how other community services help keep people safe. **Students should answer that clean water keeps people from getting sick.**

Page 57
Point out that the service industry employs about twice as many people as any other kind of job. These people work for gas stations, hotels, restaurants, hospitals, law firms, messenger services, banks, stores, computer software companies, and many other

industries. **Students should circle the woman watering the plants; they should mark an *X* on the man on the ladder.**

Page 58

Discuss some of the reasons groups of people get together to have street fairs like this one. Be sure students have correctly identified the service workers and consumers. **Students should circle baby-sitting and lawn care; they should put an *X* on people doing any three of the following: consumers paying for a necklace, a candied apple, lemonade, or a cookie; answers to the last question may include lemonade, cookies, necklaces, or candied apples.**

Page 59

Special People Explain that Hull House was known as a settlement house. Settlement houses tried to make living conditions better for immigrants in city neighborhoods. Tell students that Jane Addams got the idea for Hull House from a settlement house she visited in London, England. Then discuss some ways that people work to improve community life today. Students may be interested to know that the founding of settlement houses was only one facet of Jane Addams' social work. She was strongly interested in working to gain reforms that would benefit poor people. She organized groups that worked to get new laws passed. Addams played a key role in getting laws passed that limited the work day for women to eight hours. She was also instrumental in getting Illinois' first child-labor law passed. **Students should answer that places like Hull House help people to get to know their new community and help them meet their needs and wants.**

Page 60

Chapter Checkup You may want to work through the Chapter Checkup with students to make sure they all understand the correct answers to the numbered questions.

Answers: 1. a **2.** c **3.** c **4.** b **5.** d **6.** b
Answers will vary. After students write their answers, invite volunteers to share their observations. Be sure students emphasize that their wants are things they desire but do not need to live.

After Reading the Chapter

Discuss some of the things a smart consumer should do, such as read labels, compare prices, check warranties and return policies, and not buy things the consumer can't afford. You might bring a food product to class and teach students how to read the nutrition label. Encourage students to use these tips when they buy things.

Art
Ask students to work in small groups. Have them draw a picture map of a section of a business street or a shopping center in the community. The map should show the different kinds of stores and businesses. Tell students to label each store or business according to whether it provides goods or services.

Writing
Pose a consumer situation for students. Suggestions: the bike repair shop failed to properly fix their bike brakes, or the bike repair shop fixed the brakes and then oiled and polished the bike as well. Have students write a letter to the bike shop manager. They can either complain about the service and ask that the problem be solved or praise the shop for the extra services they received.

Drama
Have students work in small groups to perform a pantomime of someone providing a good or a service. For example, a student could mime giving another student a haircut. Have the rest of the class guess the activity and tell whether a good or service is being provided.

CHAPTER 8 — Communities Need One Another (pages 61–67)

Chapter Summary Many people are needed to produce and deliver goods. In fact, communities and even countries depend upon one another for goods. Most goods are produced in a manner that can be visualized in a flow chart. The chain of workers required to make products is effective only when each worker does his or her part.

Chapter Objectives

- explain why transportation is important in moving goods and materials from producers to consumers.
- explain why it takes many workers to produce most goods.
- explain why people in communities depend on other workers for the things they need and want.
- explain why countries around the world depend on one another.
- read flow charts and globes.

Vocabulary	
flow chart, p. 62	globe, p. 65

Vocabulary Activities Display a globe and have students locate several places, such as the United States, the Atlantic and Pacific Oceans, and various continents. Then have students take turns making up questions based on information on the globe. Other members of the class can use the globe to find the answers. Remind students that they can use the glossary to find meanings of terms they find difficult.

Before Reading the Chapter Bring to class a small selection of packaged breads from the supermarket. Ask students to speculate how the breads were transported to the supermarket and what was involved in making them. Point out that most people used to make their own bread. They also made their own clothing and tools. Today most people, especially in the United States, find it much easier and faster to buy these and other things.

Teaching Suggestions and Answers

Page 61

Remind students that they learned about goods in Chapter 5. Ask volunteers to name goods that they buy. Then ask students if the clothes they are wearing are goods. Have them look at the labels in their sweaters or jackets. Are some students wearing clothes made in other countries? **Students should answer that goods can arrive by truck, boat, and plane.**

Page 62

On a map of the United States, point out that North Dakota and Kansas are states that grow large crops of wheat. Then explain what a grain elevator is. Finally, review the sequence of steps in making bread. Explain that a flow chart shows the order in which something is done. Be sure students understand that the steps must build on one another in the right order to achieve the desired result. **Students should put an *X* on sun and soil; they should circle the wheat flowing from the elevator into the boxcar.**

Page 63

Ask students to pay close attention to the order of events. Point out that the operations shown in the pictures may take place in many different parts of the country. Ask students why they think that might be so. (geography, climate, natural resources) **Students should circle the bags of flour; they should write *truck* on the line; they should circle the Superfood store; they should answer that someone buys the bread; they should circle the checkout person and the bagger.**

Page 64

Use the flow chart on this page to illustrate to students that *all* the steps of a process must be done and must be done in the *correct order.* For instance, ask students what would happen if the chocolate and sugar were not added. Then discuss how a flow chart shows a chain of workers in action. **Students should put a checkmark under the dairy farmer milking the cow in the first step; they should put an *X* under the worker in the fourth step; they should circle the delivery person in the last step.**

Page 65

Display a globe and have students compare it to the pictures on this page. Remind students that a continent is a large land area and an ocean is a huge body of salt water. Remind students of what they learned about natural resources in Chapter 2. Then point out that the United States is lucky because it is rich in natural resources and can make most of the things it needs. Even so, our country also buys many goods from other countries. For example, we buy oil from countries in the Middle East and cars and trucks from Japan. On a map or globe locate Japan and the Middle East. **Students should circle the continental United States and Alaska; they should put an *X* on Asia.**

Project Tip

Help students carry out the suggestion on page 65. Urge students to think carefully about the goods they listed. Where did the material that went into the product come from? Was it grown? Mined? Who processed the raw material? How many steps were involved? Did people have to deliver raw materials and goods at various points along the way? Who put the product on the shelves? Who sold it? Encourage students to list as many steps as they can think of before they go to the encyclopedia.

Page 66

Around the Globe Ask students to locate Nigeria on a map of Africa. If the map is detailed enough, ask them to locate Onitsha. Explain that each woman at this market is her own boss. Her success depends on her ability to sell her products and to sell them at a profit. **Students should circle two containers in the margin photograph. They should say that farmers grow the food or the ingredients that the women use to make the food that they sell in the market.**

Page 67

Chapter Checkup To make sure all the students understand what the correct answers are to the numbered questions, work through the Chapter Checkup with the students.

Answers: 1. b **2.** b **3.** d **4.** c **5.** b **6.** c
Answers will vary. Use this question as a basis for class discussion. Urge students to explain why they would enjoy making products or providing services. Each person's thinking will help stimulate ideas in the rest of the class.

After Reading the Chapter

To help students understand the importance of a chain of workers, play a "What Happens If" game. Pose questions, such as "What happens if your bus driver is sick?", ". . . if the bread delivery truck breaks down?", ". . . if the farmer doesn't get enough rain for his wheat?" Help students to see either that other workers have to take over or that people have to do without when a link in the chain of workers breaks.

Communication

Ask students to write an explanation of how to do something that requires steps, such as making a salad or an ice cream sundae. Alternatively, you might ask students to volunteer their own ideas and explain a process with which they are familiar to the rest of the class. Remind students to use words such as *first*, *next*, *then*, and *finally* to identify each step in the process.

Geography

Ask students to survey their belongings to see which ones were produced in the United States and which ones were produced in other countries. Help students locate the other countries on a map or a globe.

Mid-term Test

The mid-term test on the following two pages covers Units 1–3, Chapters 1–8.

Answers: 1. c **2.** d **3.** c **4.** a **5.** c **6.** a **7.** c **8.** d **9.** a **10.** d **11.** a **12.** c **13.** a **14.** a **15.** c **16.** c **17.** a **18.** c **19.** a **20.** d

Name _____

Mid-Term Test

Finish each sentence. Circle the letter of the correct answer.

1. Communities are places where
   a. the government of a state meets.
   b. people buy and sell things.
   c. people live, work, and play.
   d. buildings are beautiful and old.

2. An example of a business is a
   a. city park.
   b. public library.
   c. grade school.
   d. hardware store.

3. Forests and rivers are kinds of
   a. weather.
   b. minerals.
   c. resources.
   d. landforms.

4. Most farms are located in
   a. plains.
   b. valleys.
   c. mountains.
   d. canyons.

5. Communities in rural areas are
   a. cities.
   b. capitals.
   c. towns.
   d. farms.

6. You find suburbs
   a. near big cities.
   b. near farms.
   c. near small towns.
   d. near the ocean.

7. Two kinds of transportation are
   a. houses and apartments.
   b. stores and shopping centers.
   c. cars and subways.
   d. buses and schools.

8. Communities with the biggest populations are
   a. suburbs.
   b. towns.
   c. villages.
   d. cities.

9. If you wanted to help produce goods, you could look for a job in
   a. a factory.
   b. a harbor.
   c. an apartment.
   d. a subway.

10. A political map shows
    a. shapes of the land.
    b. population.
    c. what symbols mean.
    d. borders between states and countries.

28 © Harcourt Achieve Inc. All rights reserved. Steck-Vaughn Social Studies: Living in Our Communities

Name _____

Mid-Term Test (continued)

11. You can get information about your community from
    a. interviews and old pictures.
    b. your family and your address.
    c. factories and businesses.
    d. volunteers and resources.

12. Food, clothing, and shelter are examples of
    a. goods.
    b. wants.
    c. needs.
    d. services.

13. Consumers in communities
    a. buy goods and services.
    b. work in service industries.
    c. make or grow things for sale.
    d. predict the weather.

14. To learn the steps in making a product, you could study a
    a. flow chart.
    b. globe.
    c. landform map.
    d. picture.

15. Goods are often transported by
    a. cars and buses.
    b. rivers and roads.
    c. trains and airplanes.
    d. ships and subways.

16. A globe shows
    a. state capitals.
    b. major highways.
    c. continents of the world.
    d. community resources.

17. An address tells you
    a. where you live.
    b. how old you are.
    c. how much bread costs.
    d. what time school starts.

18. Needs include
    a. books and records.
    b. dogs and cats.
    c. milk, fruit, and a house.
    d. school, stores, houses.

19. When you make something, you are called a
    a. producer.
    b. consumer.
    c. lawmaker.
    d. volunteer

20. Phillis Wheatley was an African American
    a. mayor.
    b. President.
    c. actress.
    d. poet.

© Harcourt Achieve Inc. All rights reserved. *Steck-Vaughn Social Studies: Living in Our Communities*

UNIT 4 Who Runs Our Communities? (pages 70–93)

Unit Summary All communities are run by a government. Government leaders are elected by the people in a community. Community leaders work to make and enforce laws. Laws tell people what to do and how to act. Laws also serve to protect people and to provide safety. Communities are able to provide services by collecting and using tax money.

Before Reading the Unit Introduce the unit by writing the word *leader* on the chalkboard. Ask students to tell you what they know about leaders and to give examples of leaders in their community. Write their responses on the chalkboard. Then have students read the unit opener on page 70. Encourage students to think about the unit opener questions as they read. Point out that they will learn the answers to those questions and others as they study Unit 4.

Point out the Unit Project box and tell students that they will work on this project throughout the unit.

Unit Project

Setting Up the Project It is important that students understand how an election works. Begin with a short discussion about elections. Be sure students understand that, in a democracy, people have a chance to vote for ideas or people they agree with. The idea or person who wins the most votes wins the election. The winning idea is put into practice. The winning person serves as a government leader.

Spend time discussing the importance of understanding choices in an election. There are many sides to every issue or idea. Voters need to carefully think about all sides and decide which choice is best for them and the community.

Presenting the Project One possibility is to hold a wider election among other grades. Students from each team can explain to other classes why they think their ideas will improve the school. They can advertise their ideas with posters. After the votes are tabulated, students might want to present the winning ideas to the principal.

After Reading the Unit Prompt a class discussion by asking questions such as: What are some important jobs that are done by community governments? Why are laws necessary for life in a community? Why must people pay taxes?

Skill Builder
Reading a Bar Graph

Remind students that a bar graph enables them to compare information at a glance. To reinforce this idea, ask students in which year Olive Hill had the highest population. Make sure they all understand that the longest bar in the graph shows the year in which the most people lived in Olive Hill. Remind students to read the name of the chart and the labels on the sides and at the bottom of the chart to understand the information being presented.

Answers: 1. 5,000 **2.** 1990 **3.** between 1980 and 1990 **4.** The census shows that the population of Olive Hill decreased.

Teacher's Resource Binder

Blackline Masters for Unit 4: Unit 4 Project Organizer, Unit 4 Review, Unit 4 Test; Activities for Chapters 9, 10, 11

CHAPTER 9 / Communities Have a Government (pages 71–76)

Chapter Summary Community leaders make important choices. These leaders are chosen in elections, so every person who votes has a chance to express his or her opinions. The elected leaders form the government. The government includes lawmakers, who make laws; often a mayor, who sees that laws are obeyed; and judges, who decide if laws have been broken.

Chapter Objectives Students will learn to

- explain how people in communities choose their leaders.
- read the information on a bar graph.
- identify the main function of each of the three branches of community government.

Vocabulary	
bar graph, p. 72	mayor, p. 73
government, p. 73	judge, p. 73
lawmakers, p. 73	chart, p. 74
laws, p. 73	

Vocabulary Activities Have students complete the following sentences using these vocabulary words: *government, lawmakers, mayor, judge.* A _____ sits at a tall desk in front of the court. The main leader of a city often is the _____. The job of the _____ is to make new laws for the city. These people are all members of a community's _____. If any students have difficulty with these terms, help them use the glossary to review the words.

Before Reading the Chapter If possible, arrange a display of photographs of community leaders, such as the mayor, judges, and lawmakers. Label each photograph and introduce these community leaders to the class. Ask students to share what they know about these leaders' jobs.

Teaching Suggestions and Answers

Page 71
You might play a brief game of "Follow the Leader" before students read page 71. Discuss what the role of the leader is (to make choices about what to do next). After students read page 71, you might ask them to name other ways besides voting that groups can make choices. How do they pick members for a team or decide who watches what television program? **Students should circle the American flag on the left.**

Page 72
Explain to students that American citizens must be at least 18 years old to vote in a public election. You may want to introduce the words *candidate, campaign,* and *election.* If students are familiar with these terms, you can share newspaper headlines about elections with them as you study this unit. Also ask students to tell you how the bar graph would change if they added their own vote to it. **Students should underline the words *help us get a new library.* Students should answer: the names of people running for class leader; the number of votes; 10; 8. Students should circle *Brenda* on the bar graph.**

Page 73
Point out that if elected leaders do not provide the leadership that voters want, they usually are not re-elected. You might want to explain to students that not all judges are elected by voters. Federal judges are appointed by the President and some state court judges are appointed by the state's governor. Help students find articles about government leaders in your community, and invite them to share what they learn about these leaders with the class. **Students should number the people around the table, *1*; the woman on the phone, *2*; and the judge, *3*.**

Project Tip
Help students carry out the suggestion on page 73. You might suggest that one team member serve as note taker. This person can write headings on several sheets of paper, then list the team's ideas under the appropriate headings. Urge students to think of improvements that will benefit everyone in the school, not just themselves or their class.

Page 74
Ask students why they think the mayor chooses people to fill certain community jobs. Then

discuss why larger communities might have more problems than smaller ones. Point out that larger communities have more leaders than smaller ones. **Students should circle *Health Inspector* on the chart.**

Page 75

Special People You might point out some of Jefferson's other accomplishments: Vice President under John Adams, inventor, architect, scientist, musician, and diplomat. If possible, bring in a book of photographs showing some of Jefferson's innovations. **Students will probably answer that Jefferson wrote the Declaration of Independence and served as the country's third President.**

Page 76

Chapter Checkup Make sure all students understand what the correct answers are to the numbered questions.

Answers: 1. d **2.** c **3.** a **4.** d **5.** d **6.** b
Students should answer that government leaders help communities make important decisions and choices. They may also list examples. You might want to use their examples as the basis of a wrap-up discussion on the need for community leaders.

After Reading the Chapter

You might consider arranging to take students on a field trip to your city hall or a local courtroom. If you visit city hall, be sure to point out all the departments that provide services for the community.

Writing
Have students write a letter to a community leader, inviting the person to visit your school to discuss the work he or she does. Review with students the key parts of a business letter before they begin. You might want students to write the letter as a class.

History
Have interested students ask adult acquaintances about laws that have changed their community. Have students find out when these laws were passed and why. Students can present the information to the rest of the class in a brief oral report or presentation.

Civics/Math
Have students vote on an idea such as where to go on your next field trip or what game or sport to play in gym class. Give students two choices to vote for. Have volunteers tally the votes and write the counts on the board. Provide students with graph paper and have them show the results of the vote in a bar graph.

History
Have students work with a partner to make a chart of United States Presidents. In the first column of their chart, students should write the names of three or four Presidents; in the second column, they should write an important fact about each of the Presidents. Display students' charts in the classroom.

Social Studies
Divide the class into small groups. Tell each group to imagine that they are starting a new community. Ask them to think of three laws that would be important for a new community to establish. Have a volunteer from each group explain to the class their group's laws and the reasons for the laws.

CHAPTER 10 — Communities Have Rules and Laws (pages 77–83)

Chapter Summary Rules and laws are necessary for community life. They help guide our actions and tell us what is fair. Laws are community rules. The purpose of many laws is to keep people safe and healthy.

Chapter Objectives Students will learn to

- explain why communities have rules and laws.
- list examples of rules and laws.
- identify some community workers who help to enforce rules and laws.

Vocabulary
census, p. 82

Vocabulary Activities Take a sample census. Help students develop a fictitious family. Have students think of the number of members in the family and decide how many are children and how many are adults. Have students also list the children's ages. Ask students what other information they would like to include on the census form before it is finalized. Then have students fill out the form, tally the results, and decide how to present the information. Ask them how this information might be used by a lawmaker to benefit the students and their families. Help students use the glossary if they seem to have difficulty with any of the terms.

Before Reading the Chapter Invite students to discuss situations in which someone did not play by the rules. Ask them to describe several situations. What were the outcomes? How did others feel? Work with students to understand the importance of fairness in both work and play, and how fairness makes achievements and good will possible.

Teaching Suggestions and Answers
Page 77
Hold a discussion about different kinds of rules. Use the following to prompt the students: Name some rules you know in games or sports. Name some rules concerning politeness. Name some important school rules. **Students should put an X on the girl on the right.**

Page 78
Introduce the concept of cause and effect. Discuss the examples of cause and effect on this page. Then ask students to think of other examples. Write their ideas on the board under the headings *Cause* and *Effect,* connecting them with arrows, or use the Cause and Effect graphic organizer found on page 64 of this guide. **Students should put an X on the first girl on the left; they should circle the girl on the far right; they should write *Don't litter*.**

Page 79
Point out to students that rules and laws change constantly. Throughout history people have invented new laws and rules as different needs arose or as lawmakers recognized a current law as not being fair. Mention that until the early 1900s, it was against the law for women to vote. Mention also that before the 1960s, there were very few laws about environmental pollution. Explain to students that laws touch nearly every area of our lives. You might list a few examples, such as laws about where and how long to park cars; laws about selling goods and medicines; laws that control what businesses can do. After students read this page, review the safety procedures for cars and pedestrians near your school. **Students should circle the 55 MPH sign; they should write *SLOW School Crossing* on the line; they should draw an arrow pointing to the green light on the traffic light.**

Project Tip
Help students carry out the suggestion on page 79. You may want to suggest topics to get students started. These might include rules about noise, clothes, behavior in the classroom and in the hall, and personal belongings.

Page 80
Ask students to name other ways in which drivers might break the law. Examples include driving through a stop light and going the wrong way on a one-way street. Then discuss with students why traffic laws are important. Discuss with students

road signs that use pictures to tell people about a rule. If possible, show or draw them some examples of these signs such as the "no U-turn" or "no bicycles" signs. Ask students what advantages these types of signs have over worded signs (such signs can be universally understood even by people who are too young to read or who don't speak English). **Students should circle the 15 MPH sign; they should write** *It's a school zone.*

Page 81

Explain to students that if foods are not kept cold, bacteria can grow in them. Bacteria can also grow in places that are not kept clean. Some bacteria cause illnesses. Also point out that vaccinations prevent diseases that spread easily and cause serious illness. Ask students to think of some rules that concern health (covering the mouth when sneezing or coughing, washing hands before meals). **Students should put an *X* on the man in the picture. They should write that the other person is washing dishes.**

Page 82

For Your Information Explain that the most recent census was taken in 2000. The next one will be taken in 2010. Also tell the class that money from the U.S. government is often given to states depending on their population needs. **Students should circle the red area on the map.**

Page 83

Chapter Checkup You may want to work through the Chapter Checkup with students.

Answers: 1. b **2.** d **3.** c **4.** a **5.** c **6.** b
Answers will vary, but will probably deal with traffic rules. Ask volunteers to share their answers. List them on the chalkboard.

After Reading the Chapter

Take students on a "law walk" through a day of their lives. Discuss how laws affect nearly everything they do, starting with breakfast. For instance, laws affect the ingredients of cereal and other packaged foods.

Art
Students can create safety posters to hang in the school hallways. You might suggest that they discuss the biggest school safety problems with the principal, crossing guards, or custodians.

Writing
Display a picture of a car. Tell students that 100 years ago there were no laws about cars because there were very few cars then. Guide the class in understanding that often laws are made as the need arises. Show students a picture of a computer. Invite students to write several new laws that this invention might require.

Reading
Have students check local newspapers for articles about community rules and laws. Ask students to bring in the articles for a bulletin board display about laws in the community.

Health
Invite the school nurse to visit and speak to the class about preventive medicine. He or she should explain why there are laws requiring immunization against certain diseases such as diphtheria, tetanus, whooping cough, and polio. The nurse might also explain how immunization has dramatically reduced the number of deaths due to infectious diseases.

Writing
Point out to students that many rules are written with a negative in them: Don't Walk on the Grass; No Running in the Halls. Have students make a list of other negative rules. Then challenge the students to rewrite the rules in a more positive way. For example: You May Walk Around the Grass; Please Walk in the Halls.

CHAPTER 11 / Communities Provide Services (pages 84–91)

Chapter Summary Communities provide schools, water, electricity, firefighters, police officers, consumer protection, roads, buildings, and other services for their citizens. People pay for these services with taxes. The number of services varies according to the size of a community.

Chapter Objectives Students will learn to

- list examples of the kinds of services a community provides.
- explain how communities pay for the services they provide.
- identify reasons why people in communities need various services.
- explain why the number of services varies with the size of a community.

Vocabulary

tax, p. 86

Vocabulary Activities Begin a word web on the chalkboard with the word *tax*. Explain that taxes come from the money that workers pay to the community from the wages they earn. Also explain that communities use tax money to pay for things the community needs and wants, such as traffic lights, new park benches, and traffic police. As students read the chapter, have them expand the web by adding more needs and wants.

Before Reading the Chapter Review the community workers that students have already studied and discuss briefly what they do and why they are important to the community. Ask students to name other workers and predict whether they are community workers.

Teaching Suggestions and Answers
Page 84
Explain that the services a community provides are public services. Ask students to name those who use public services (anyone who lives in the community). Discuss the importance of the city services mentioned on this page. **Students should circle the teacher in the photograph.**

Page 85
Ask students to study the picture on this page and name the workers shown in the picture. Ask them why these people are working in a group. (They depend on each other to do the job.) Work with students to compile a list of different kinds of workers in your school. **Students should shade the hat of the worker standing on the second level; they should circle the worker laying bricks on the bottom level; they should put an X on the man kneeling on the second level.**

Page 86
Remind students that voters choose the leaders who decide how to spend tax money for the community. Sometimes these leaders decide whether taxes should be raised or lowered to meet a community's needs. Many factors affect how a community spends the taxes it collects. The location of a community is one factor. For example, a community in northern Minnesota gets a lot of snow in the winter. That community uses some of its taxes to buy snow-removal equipment, keep the equipment maintained, and pay the workers who operate the equipment. A community in southern Florida that never gets snow would spend its taxes on different services. Taxes might go toward maintaining public beaches and paying lifeguards. **Students should put a checkmark under the box at the top of the flow chart; they should circle the box southeast of the top box that reads: WORKERS GIVE UP PART OF THEIR PAY AS TAXES.**

Page 87
Explain that because big cities have more or different needs than small communities, they have more services. For instance, big city airports have big terminals because so many people fly in and out of the cities on business, vacations, and so on. Many major cities also have special terminals for travelers from other countries. These airports also have more workers and equipment for emergencies. **Answers will vary. Students should provide two examples of services in their community.**

Project Tip
Help students carry out the suggestion on page 87. Point out that tax money can be spent on things, such as computers and books; or on people, such as teachers, librarians, and office workers. Suggest that students take turns taking notes.

Page 88
Explain that consumer inspectors check to see that consumer laws are met. They also decide whether consumers are being charged a fair price for products and services. Discuss common consumer problems and procedures, such as returning items. **Students' answers should include snow plowing; they should write that consumer inspectors make sure that consumers are charged fair prices.**

Page 89
Review with students the problem presented in each picture. After students complete this page, have volunteers role-play an emergency telephone call for a fire, an accident, or an illness. Discuss the information they should give.
In picture A, a thief is breaking into a store. Students should make the following line connections: A-4; B-2; C-3; D-1.

Page 90
Around the Globe Have students locate Mexico on a map of North America or the world. Then explain that in order for the people of Las Palomas and Columbus to go from town to town, they must cross an international border checkpoint. Also point out that the language of Mexico is Spanish. Most people along both sides of the border speak both Spanish and English. **Students should circle Las Palomas and underline Columbus; they should put a checkmark next to Mexico on the map. Their answers to the last question will vary, but may include health services, street repair and lighting, and teachers.**

Page 91
Chapter Checkup Work through the Chapter Checkup with students. Make sure they all understand what the correct answers are to the numbered questions.
Answers: 1. c **2.** b **3.** d **4.** a **5.** b **6.** d
Answers will vary, but may include problems of garbage pickup, consumer protection, police and fire protection, emergency hospital care, snow removal, and education. Urge volunteers to share their answers so that students have a sense of the full range of community services paid for by taxes.

After Reading the Chapter
Discuss the difference between private and public services. Make sure students understand that private services are provided directly to the people who use them, while public services are paid for with public money and are shared by the community. Ask students to draw a picture of one private service and one community service.

Social Studies
Have students use the Yellow Pages to make a list of departments and services in their community government. In discussion, ask what information they found most surprising.

Writing
Have students write a list of emergency numbers they can use at home. The lists might include 911, their doctor's number, their dentist's number, parents' work numbers, numbers for neighbors, an electrician, plumber, and so on. You might have students write a brief message they would give if they had to make an emergency call, including their name, address, telephone number, and a description of what happened.

Art
Have groups of students work together to make a poster promoting a community service. For example, students might choose to encourage citizens to take advantage of a community park or beach or to participate in the community's recycling program.

UNIT 5 Communities Change (pages 94–119)

Unit Summary Communities change over time. One such community is Omaha, Nebraska. The earliest people to live in this area were the Omaha. Their way of life depended on the land. In the 1800s, pioneers founded a community named for the Omaha. The city's central location helped it grow. Today, Omaha is a large city coping with many of the problems of other large cities.

Before Reading the Unit Introduce the unit by asking students to imagine life without telephones, televisions, cars, paved roads, buses, trains, tall buildings, or even very many cities. How would you get from place to place? How would you communicate with friends? Point out that about 250 years ago, all of America was like this. Most of the communities that did exist were American Indian communities.

Next, ask a volunteer to read the unit opener aloud. Then have students locate Omaha, Nebraska on a United States map. Ask students to look at the photograph. Ask: How can you tell Omaha is a large city? Encourage students to use the unit opener questions as guides for their reading. Explain that they will learn the answers to these questions and others as they study Unit 5.

Point out the Unit Project box. Explain to students that they will work on this project as they read through the unit.

Unit Project

Setting Up The Project Students will find their end product most gratifying if they locate a rich variety of visual information and details about their community. Local sources will be able to provide most of the information students need. However, you might also suggest that students ask their families if they have any old pictures of the community they could borrow or copy. Also emphasize the importance of getting as many precise dates of events as possible. Local brochures may have chronologies that students can use to develop their time line.

Presenting the Project Students can follow the suggestions on page 119 or paint pictures of several community locations as they were in the past and as they look today. The pictures could form the basis of a bulletin board display called "Yesterday and Today." Students may add pictures showing their vision of tomorrow.

After Reading the Unit Discuss the unit opener questions and the answers students discovered. Prompt the discussion by asking questions such as: Can new people change a community? How? How can new industries change a community? Give an example.

Skill Builder

Using a Diagram

Remind students that a diagram is a picture with labels that shows how something works or how something is made. Ask students to look at the diagram on page 118 and describe the landforms and natural resources found where the Tlingit lived. Students should indicate that mountains are landforms and that forests, animals, and water are resources.

Answers: 1. Students should add the label to the plank house. **2.** Students should circle the totem pole, plank houses, or canoe. **3.** fish and deer meat **4.** totem poles

Teacher's Resource Binder

Blackline Masters for Unit 5: Unit 5 Project Organizer, Unit 5 Review, Unit 5 Test; Activities for Chapters 12, 13, 14; Outline Maps of the United States and the World

CHAPTER 12 / American Indian Communities (pages 95–103)

Chapter Summary The Omaha people of present-day Nebraska lived in earth lodges made of logs and blocks of soil and grass. Near their lodges they farmed and they fished. Part of the year the Omaha traveled west on horseback to hunt buffalo. The buffalo supplied them with meat, hides for clothing, blankets, shoes, and portable tepees.

Chapter Objectives Students will learn to

- use a distance scale on a map.
- describe an early Omaha community in Nebraska.
- interpret a diagram.
- explain the importance of buffalo to the Omaha people.
- list some of the problems the Omaha faced.

Vocabulary
earth lodges, p. 96   tepees, p. 99
diagram, p. 98

Vocabulary Activities Help students build a word web about different kinds of shelter. Point out that the earth lodges of the Omaha people are one kind of shelter people used in the past. Students can include examples of shelters from the past or present. Remind students to use the glossary if they seem to have difficulty with any of the terms.

Before Reading the Chapter Have students turn to the map of the United States on page 137. Help them trace the route of the Missouri River as it flows from South Dakota along the eastern border of Nebraska and into Missouri, where it finally joins the Mississippi River. Discuss rivers as transportation routes. Remind students that many communities developed along rivers.

Teaching Suggestions and Answers
Page 95
Point out that the map shows the states as they exist now. Ask students to look at the map and name what was on the eastern edge of the Omaha's territory (Mississippi River). **Students should estimate that it was roughly 750 miles across Omaha land.**

Page 96
Point out that the base of an earth lodge is made in a circle. Ask students to name the materials their homes are made of. **Students should complete the circle and draw vertical lines to show the placement of wall logs.**

Page 97
Tell students that the storage hole in the earth lodge was called a cache. Remind students that the Omaha built their homes with materials they found around them. Ask students why they think we now have to ship many different materials and supplies to the sites where new homes are being built. (Many of the materials used to build houses today are manufactured products such as bricks, plastic, vinyl, aluminum, and glass and must be purchased. People no longer make houses from what can be found nearby.) **Students should say that men showed where the walls would be and put the logs in place, and that women dug the floor and made the roof and the storage hole; they should put an *X* in front of and to one side of the doorway.**

Page 98
Discuss with students how living in villages helped the Omaha get food. Ask students to compare ways in which we travel now to the ways in which the Omaha traveled. Tell students that before the 1600s, the Omaha and other American Indians of the Great Plains did not have horses. The horses were brought to the region by European explorers. Horses dramatically changed the lives of the Plains Indians. Having horses made it much easier to follow herds of buffalo. The Omaha and other Plains Indians became expert horse riders. **Students should draw a line under the word *fields*; they should circle the label *earth lodge*.**

Page 99
Point out that tepees were ideal for traveling. The Omaha could take them down quickly and easily when they had to move. They took the

poles and the buffalo-skin shelters with them. Explain to students how the Omaha set up their tepees. **Students should circle a tepee.**

Page 100

Explain to students that the Omaha often spent days tracking the buffalo before they could hunt them. Tell students that many Plains Indians used buffalo in pemmican—thin slices of dried, cooked meat mixed with berries and fat. They used buffalo horns for spoons and ladles; they used bone for tools; hair was used to braid bridles for the horses. **Students should answer that the Omaha could move as fast as the buffalo when they rode on horses.**

Page 101

Have students look at the illustration at the bottom of the page. Tell students that the dog is pulling a *travois*—a sledlike platform. The Omaha and other Plains Indians used travois to haul buffalo meat. **Students should circle the dog and horses.**

Project Tip

Help students carry out the suggestion on page 101. You may want to suggest that students ask the local community librarian or a person at the local historical society to help them locate information. Team members may want to divide the work and seek facts from different sources.

Page 102

Special People Explain to students that settlers from Europe and the eastern colonies came to Cherokee and Omaha land and began to settle there. Before they came, there had been no one but American Indians on the land for a long, long time. Also explain that before Sequoyah's "talking leaves," the Cherokee passed stories on by telling them to one another. Discuss the advantages and disadvantages of an oral versus a written tradition. **Students should say that a written language allowed the Cherokee to have a written record of their traditions.**

Page 103

Chapter Checkup Make sure all students understand what the correct answers are to the numbered questions.

Answers: **1.** b **2.** d **3.** a **4.** c **5.** c **6.** a
Students will say that the buffalo were used for food, clothing, and shelter—thus meeting all the Omaha's needs.

After Reading the Chapter

Divide the class into two groups and have them make a chart comparing the Omaha way of life with their way of life. Headings might include shelter, storage, clothing, and transportation. Students may also compare how people obtain food, what foods they eat, the roles of men and women, and community problems.

Art

Ask students to research another American Indian group and make a diagram showing some aspect of how they lived. Students can focus on shelters, clothing, tools, or any other subject that interests them.

Communication

Tell students that the Omaha belonged to a larger related group of American Indians known as the Plains Indians. Because the different groups that lived on the Great Plains all spoke different languages, they invented a sign language, which groups used to communicate with one another. Have students work in small groups to devise a sign language of their own for a few words. Suggest that students start out by creating signs for the vocabulary terms *earth lodges* and *tepees*.

CHAPTER 13 / Early Communities (pages 104–110)

Chapter Summary In the mid-1800s, American pioneers moved into Omaha land in covered wagons. They settled on Omaha land. In 1854 they founded the community of Omaha near the Missouri River. Omaha grew because of its location near rich farm land and its access to steamboat traffic on the Missouri River. Varied industries grew, including brick-making and lumber-milling. With the coming of the railroad in the 1860s, Omaha became a center for meatpacking and grain mills, and its population continued to grow.

Chapter Objectives Students will learn to

- explain why pioneers traveled west to form new communities.
- describe how and why the population of Omaha changed over time.
- explain the importance of good transportation to a community's growth.
- read a grid map and a time line.

Vocabulary	
pioneers, p. 104	time line, p. 107
industries, p. 106	grid, p. 108

Vocabulary Activities Write the word *industry* in a sentence on the chalkboard. Ask students if they can name some major industries in your community. List these industries on the chalkboard. If students know someone who works in a particular industry, they might describe the person's job to the class. Advise students to use the glossary if they have difficulty with any of the terms.

Before Reading the Chapter Ask students to describe the land where the Omaha lived. Then point out the map on page 105. Explain the different roads and trails. Remind students that wagon roads were not paved 150 years ago. Even today, you can see ruts in the ground left by thousands of wagon trains traveling west. You might want to read aloud from *Women's Diaries of the Westward Journey* by Lillian Schlissel to give students a sense of the pioneer experience. Explain that the Pony Express was not a wagon trail, but a route used for a short time by mail carriers traveling on fast horses.

Teaching Suggestions and Answers
Page 104
Discuss with students why the pioneers wanted new land to farm. You might explain that by the mid-1800s, eastern cities were getting crowded and most of the best farm land in the East and Midwest had been taken. **Students should circle the covered wagons in the picture.**

Page 105
Ask students to identify the main transportation routes that passed through Omaha. Have them name things the pioneers might have needed for the trip. To help students practice reading a map key, ask students to trace one route that people traveled, and one route that cattle traveled. **Students should circle Omaha.**

Page 106
Tell students that this picture of Omaha was taken in 1863. Ask them to name some things that come from cattle, such as meat and leather. **Students should circle one of the stores in the photo.**

Page 107
Be sure students understand that a time line shows events in the order they happened and that they should read a time line from left to right. To provide practice working with a time line, ask students to calculate the number of years that passed between the year Omaha became capital and the year the capital moved from Omaha to Lincoln, Nebraska (12 years). Discuss the reasons a railroad was needed to link the east and west coasts. Point out that towns along railroads grew quickly because industries in those towns could ship their goods out and bring supplies in by railroad. Point out that cattle were often kept in pens next to the railroad yard so they could be loaded onto trains quickly and easily. **Students should answer 11 years.**

Page 108

Tell students that the map shows how Omaha looked in 1866. Explain that as Omaha grew, it spread north, south, and west. Have students look at the map. Ask them why Omaha did not grow eastward. **Students should say the Missouri River. They should color the entire length of the Missouri River on the map.**

Project Tip

Help students carry out the suggestion on page 108. Tell students that the public library and local historical society can help them find this information. Community organizations may have brochures with pictures of the community's early years. Remind students to get as many exact dates as they can, such as the date the community was founded, the dates important businesses began, and the dates when important transportation links were built.

Page 109

For Your Information You might point out that the first pioneers to settle in Nebraska were given the nickname, "sodbusters." There were so few trees that the pioneers had to cut the grassy earth (sod) into blocks to use as "bricks" to build their houses. Later, Nebraska became known as the "tree planters' state" because the pioneers planted so many trees. Discuss with students why farming in Nebraska is important to the whole country. **Students should say that Major Long was wrong to think Nebraska was a desert that could not be farmed. In fact, it was good land for raising cattle and growing crops.**

Page 110

Chapter Checkup You may want to work through the Chapter Checkup with the students. Make sure they all understand what the correct answers are to the numbered questions.

Answers: 1. c **2.** b **3.** c **4.** a **5.** b **6.** b
Students will say that trains brought cattle to Omaha. A meat-packing industry started, so many new jobs opened up. Trains also brought grains to Omaha. New mills were built and people came to Omaha to work in the mills. Ask several students to share their answers.

After Reading the Chapter

Have students look again at the painting on page 104. Ask them to list things that they think the pioneers carried in their covered wagons. Point out that some items, such as the kettle and washtub, are shown in the picture.

Writing

Ask students to imagine they are pioneers in long-ago Omaha. Have them write a journal entry about a day in the life of a pioneer child. You might suggest they look at the painting on page 104 or the photograph on page 106 for ideas.

History

Invite students to interview family members or family friends who remember how the community looked many decades ago. Have them write what they learn and create a pamphlet about the community's past. Students may illustrate their pamphlets with photographs.

Social Studies

Show students the route of the Pony Express on the map on page 105. Invite interested students to find out about the role the Pony Express played in communications and the settlement of Nebraska and the American frontier. Ask students to share their findings with the rest of the class by giving an informal oral report.

CHAPTER 14 / Communities Grow (pages 111–117)

Chapter Summary Today, Omaha is the largest city in Nebraska. Its main industries are food processing, trucking, computer work, and telemarketing. As Omaha grew, people moved out of the old parts of the city and into new ones. Old areas became run down. In recent years, some of these areas have been restored and are now centers for shopping and dining.

Chapter Objectives Students will learn to

- name some important industries in Omaha today.

- identify a problem that many cities have as they get larger and older.

- describe how a city can solve the problem of run-down buildings.

- compare Omaha of the past with Omaha of today.

Vocabulary
future, p. 114

Vocabulary Activities Write the word *future* on the chalkboard. Ask students to name the opposite of the future (past). Then ask students to discuss why it might be important to think about the future today. For instance, ask students if tomorrow is the future. Ask what things they must do today to prepare for events tomorrow. Point out that the things we do today can shape and change many of our tomorrows.

Before Reading the Chapter Discuss how new inventions bring change. Have students name some appliances or machines they use at home. Then ask them to speculate on what people did before these things were invented. Tell students that pioneers took four to six months to travel the 2,000 miles of the Oregon Trail. Today, people can fly that same distance in four or five hours.

Teaching Suggestions and Answers
Page 111
Point out that trucks had not been invented 100 years ago. Help students think of other industries that also did not exist 100 years ago, such as computer work and telemarketing. **Students may answer: by airplane, train, or ship.**

Page 112
Be sure students understand that residential areas are not the only areas that can become run down. Many large cities, including Omaha, have seen their downtown business districts suffer in recent years. In some cases, businesses and city government work together to beautify and restore downtown business areas. Point out that while some areas in Omaha declined, others were still thriving. The whole city did not become run down at once. Ask students why streets would get dirty after people moved away. **Students' answers may include: the paint peels off; windows break; the roof leaks; the house starts to fall apart.**

Project Tip
Help students carry out the suggestion on page 112. Point students to a variety of sources for this information, such as recent newspapers and other community publications, family snapshots, and pictures students draw. Have teams brainstorm other sources as well.

Page 113
Point out that buildings that once housed industries or served as warehouses are sometimes used for different purposes now. In many cities, these big, well-built buildings have been turned into apartments, stores, offices, and art galleries. Ask students if they know of any local buildings that have been fixed up. **Students should answer that the buildings have been fixed up; they are well-kept, have new signs, and new shops.**

Page 114
Point out to students that the map of Omaha at the bottom of the page is a grid map. Review with students how to use a grid map. Ask: In what grid is the Henry Doorly Zoo? (C-3) In which grid are the warehouses? (C-2) Ask students to name some reasons that people leave a city. Then ask them to think about future changes that might affect Omaha. Topics to consider include transportation, industry, and communications. **Students' answers may include:**

42

Omaha spread north, south, and west; a high school was built; a zoo and an airport were built.

Page 115

Tell students that one of the photographs shows Omaha in 1880. Discuss with students how some businesses become less important over time. For instance, Omaha doesn't need wagon-wheel repair shops now because people drive cars. **Students' answers may include: Omaha now has paved roads; Omaha now has skyscrapers.**

Page 116

Around the Globe Ask students to find Mexico on a world map. Then have them locate Mexico City. Explain that Mexicans are no longer ruled by the Spanish, although Mexican people speak Spanish. Tell students that many people who live in Mexico have Aztec ancestors. Evidence of the Aztec civilization remains in Mexico today. Several Aztec buildings near Mexico City have been restored by archaeologists. The words *chocolate, avocado,* and *tomato* came from the Aztec language. Chili, tacos, and chocolate are foods that were eaten by the Aztecs and are today enjoyed by people in many countries of the world. **Students should circle the Spanish church; they should put an *X* on a new building.**

Page 117

Chapter Checkup Work through the Chapter Checkup with students to be sure they all understand what the correct answers are to the numbered questions.

Answers: 1. d **2.** b **3.** b **4.** b **5.** c **6.** c
Answers will vary widely. Ask volunteers to share their answers with the class so that many different points of view are aired.

After Reading the Chapter

Discuss other problems that communities face in addition to run-down buildings. What problems does your community face? What are some possible solutions? Remind the class that people in a community often vote for leaders who promise to help solve community problems.

Art
Ask students to think about the future of your community. Then have them design and make a mural showing how their community will look in 25 years.

Writing
After students have finished the chapter, and have a sense of how communities change, suggest they write their thoughts about how change can benefit or hurt a community. They should write freely, reflecting all their thoughts about how community change can be a good thing or an upsetting thing.

Geography
Have students study the grid map of Omaha on page 114. Invite students to make a simple grid map of their neighborhood or the area surrounding the school. Students may want to work in small cooperative groups for this activity. Advise students to draw the map first and then add the grid. Have students practice using the grid to locate different places on the map.

Social Studies
Have students interview some adults about important changes or events that have taken place in their community. Students may find out when their school was built, when certain businesses opened, when a mayor was elected, and so forth. Have students take notes about the events and the year the events took place. Students should use their findings to make a class time line about the community.

UNIT 6 — Communities Share (pages 120–136)

Unit Summary Every community in America is different, but all of America's communities share many things. They are all part of one nation and share one national government. Americans also share the same capital in Washington, D.C. American communities celebrate many of the same national holidays and share the freedom to preserve the national and ethnic heritages of the people who live in our communities.

Before Reading the Unit You might want to introduce this unit by having the class recite the Pledge of Allegiance. Explain that this is one way that Americans honor their country and their shared nationhood. Then have the class read the unit opener on page 120 and discuss the questions and the photograph. You might ask what shared celebration the photograph probably shows (Fourth of July). Encourage students to use the questions as guides as they read. They will learn the answers to these questions and others as they study Unit 6. Point out the Unit Project box. Tell students that they will work on this project as they read through the unit.

Unit Project

Setting Up the Project In order for students to find enough pictures for their display, they need to think about the variety of things made in this country. You might launch the project with a class brainstorming session. Start off by telling students that the hot dog, the automobile, and the airplane were invented in the United States. Ask students what other things have been made here. You might write headings on the chalkboard, such as *Foods, Clothing, Tools, Transportation,* and so on. Tell students they can find pictures for their displays in newspapers, magazines, and calendars. Urge students to thumb through photography books at the library and draw pictures of some of the most interesting items they find.

Presenting the Project One additional possibility might be to have students organize their pictures and facts into a mock public television show. Students could find tapes of American folk songs, jazz, and other music to play in the background. They could write an introduction, then each present one interesting object and its story.

After Reading the Unit Invite discussion of the unit opener questions with these prompts: In what ways is Washington, D.C. our city? In what ways do all Americans celebrate together?

Skill Builder

Using a Chart
As students read page 135, remind them that charts enable you to compare similar facts about different things quickly. To illustrate this, ask students which row of information on the chart tells the month in which festivals are held in four communities. Note that at a glance they can see that the festivals are in March, April, and July.

Answers: 1. Chasco Fiesta **2.** Tulip Festival **3.** Traverse City, Michigan **4.** Kōloa Plantation Days and the Cherry Festival

Teacher's Resource Binder

Blackline Masters for Unit 6: Unit 6 Project Organizer, Unit 6 Review, Unit 6 Test; Activities for Chapters 14 and 15; Outline Map of the United States

CHAPTER 15 / Our Nation's Capital (pages 121–127)

Chapter Summary Washington, D.C., is our national capital, a community all Americans share. Our national government in Washington, D.C. consists of three branches—the President, the Congress, and the Supreme Court. The President and Congress are elected. Washington, D.C. is named for George Washington, the nation's first President. The city is full of statues honoring other important Americans. Washington is also home to the Library of Congress and the Smithsonian Institution, which preserves and showcases our heritage.

Chapter Objectives Students will learn to

- explain the functions of the President, Congress, and Supreme Court.
- list some important buildings in Washington, D.C.
- explain why Washington, D.C., is important to all Americans.
- explain how Washington, D.C., got its name.
- use a chart.

Vocabulary	
elected, p. 122	Supreme Court, p. 123
Congress, p. 122	

Vocabulary Activities Write *President, Congress,* and *Supreme Court* on the chalkboard. Discuss with students what each of these branches of the national government do. Then ask students to name their counterparts at the community level. Write *mayor* or other main community leader, *lawmakers,* and *judges* beneath the parallel words. If any students have difficulty with these terms, help them use the glossary for review.

Before Reading the Chapter Ask students to watch the television news for current information about the President of the United States. Have them keep a record of what he says and does over several days or a week. Ask students to report on what they heard. Discuss the President's actions with the class.

Teaching Suggestions and Answers

Page 121
Ask students to locate Washington, D.C., on a map of the United States. Have a volunteer identify the current President. **Students' answers may include: because the President is an important person; because Americans are proud of their President.**

Page 122
Ask students why they think we need lawmakers for the whole country, not just our individual communities. Also ask students to name some issues Congress might decide. Have students explain why members of Congress discuss issues before they vote. **Students should properly identify the Capitol and write *Congress* next to the picture.**

Page 123
Explain to students that there are different kinds of courts in this country. The Supreme Court makes decisions about laws that affect the whole nation. Lower courts make decisions about community and state laws. **Students should underline Congress; they should circle President; they should put an *X* on Supreme Court.**

Page 124
Discuss other ways that important people are honored. For example, some of our famous Presidents (Washington, Lincoln, Jefferson) are featured on paper money and coins. Postage stamps also often picture Presidents or other important government leaders. Then ask students to turn back to page 122. Point out that the large building on the right side of the photograph behind the Capitol is the Library of Congress. Tell students that Thomas Jefferson's personal library of 6,000 books formed the basis of the Library of Congress collection in 1815. **Students' answers will vary. Some may say he looks serious because he had such big problems to solve and he was in office during a sad time in our country's history.**

45

Page 125

Tell students that the Smithsonian museums have about 100 million objects in their collections, including art, historical objects, fossils, jewels, airplanes, and spacecraft. Among the treasures are the Hope Diamond, the largest blue diamond in the world, and the original Teddy Bear made in 1903. Ask students to discuss the reasons it is important to save so many things. **Students' answers may include because these things belong to all Americans and Washington, D.C., is everyone's city.**

Project Tip

Help students carry out the suggestion on page 125. Urge teams to refer to the ideas from the class brainstorming session, then have a brief brainstorming session of their own. Students should decide in advance if every team member will search for a variety of images or whether each person will look for pictures in just one category.

Page 126

Special People Discuss with students the difference a woman justice might make on the Supreme Court. Tell students that Sandra Day O'Connor is no longer the only female Supreme Court Justice. Ruth Bader Ginsburg was appointed to the Supreme Court in 1993 by President Bill Clinton. **Students should answer 1981.**

Page 127

Chapter Checkup Make sure all students understand what the correct answers are to the numbered questions.

Answers: 1. c **2.** b **3.** b **4.** c **5.** a **6.** d
Answers will vary. Students should say that both have leaders, people who make laws, and courts that decide if laws have been broken. Ask volunteers if they have any other ideas. Some students may also say that both governments are made up largely of people who are elected. Others may point out that state and national governments meet in capital cities.

After Reading the Chapter

Have students make a travel poster advertising Washington, D.C. They can gather information about Washington, D.C., in the library and write for information from the Washington, D.C., Convention and Tourism Corporation, 901 7th Street, NW, 4th Fl., Washington, DC 20001-3719. Students can cut out pictures from brochures. They may wish to make a map featuring all the historical places and other places of interest that visitors to the city might want to see. Encourage students to come up with a slogan for their poster.

Writing

Help the class write a letter to one of your state senators or representatives in Congress, asking for information about a local matter of interest to students.

Art

Have students draw pictures of other things Americans share. Examples might be our flag; the kinds of the places we shop (malls); television shows we watch; historic events we share, such as the moon landing or the inauguration of a new President; even the clothing we wear and the money we spend.

Social Studies

Provide students with picture books about Washington, D.C. and a large-scale map of the capital. Have students work in groups to plan a trip to Washington. Groups should make up an itinerary and identify some of their destinations on the map.

CHAPTER 16 / Communities Celebrate (pages 128–134)

Chapter Summary This chapter describes the holidays and traditions that bind us together as a people while respecting our individuality. American traditions have a long history. The first Thanksgiving celebrated the Pilgrims' gratitude for good crops. Thanksgiving became a national holiday in 1863. Independence Day celebrates America's freedom from Great Britain, which occurred in 1776. America also honors the traditions people bring to the country, including Chinese New Year, fiesta, and Trung Thu, a Vietnamese children's celebration.

Chapter Objectives Students will learn to

- list some holidays that Americans share.
- explain why Thanksgiving and Independence Day are important.
- explain what a tradition is.
- list examples of different kinds of American traditions.

Vocabulary

celebrate, p. 128   fiesta, p. 132
tradition, p. 129

Vocabulary Activities Work with students to build a word web showing examples of traditions. Write *American traditions* at the center of the web. As students read the chapter, have them name different traditions to add to the web. Follow up by having students draw pictures of the traditions they like best.

Before Reading the Chapter Ask students to name their favorite holidays. Have them describe the things they like most about these occasions. Help students find the date for each holiday on a calendar. Then have them illustrate the holidays for a bulletin-board display.

Teaching Suggestions and Answers
Page 128
Review with the class why the Pilgrims came to America and how difficult their first year in the new land was. Tell students that, in addition to some of the foods shown in the illustration of the first Thanksgiving, the Pilgrims probably also ate deer, eels, clams, nuts, corn, and berries. Invite students to tell about their own Thanksgiving traditions. Ask: What foods does your family prepare? Who cooks? Some students may volunteer to share information about ethnic dishes or traditions that are part of their holiday. **Students' answers may include pumpkin and carrots.**

Page 129
Discuss how the Pilgrims got their food—by hunting, fishing, gathering wild berries, and farming. Ask students to think of other American traditions they observe. **Students' answers will vary.**

Project Tip
Help students carry out the suggestion on page 129. Students can offer facts and pictures of their own cultural traditions, but urge them to explore the traditions of other cultures, too.

Page 130
Remind students that the United States fought for its freedom from Great Britain in the American Revolutionary War. Discuss how your community celebrates the Fourth of July. **Students should circle the American flags in the photograph. Their answers may include: because of all the flags.**

Page 131
Explain that Chinese New Year parades are held in many large cities of the United States. The photograph in the text shows a parade in New York City, but San Francisco is also famous for its Chinese New Year parade. Ask volunteers to share information about their cultural heritages with the class. **Students should put an X on the man wearing the dragon mask in the photograph.**

Page 132
Ask students to find San Antonio, Texas, on a map of the United States, and Vietnam on a map of the world. You might tell students that on

Trung Thu, people eat delicious moon cakes made with nuts and fruits and carry lanterns, many shaped like the moon. This is because Trung Thu also celebrates the beautiful full moon of the fall. You might tell students that Japan also has special holidays for children. During the Girls' Festival in March and the Boys' Festival in May, families display dolls that have been passed down from generation to generation. The girls' dolls are dressed like Japan's emperors and empresses and the boys' dolls are warriors and heroes. During the festivals, children learn about Japan's history, culture, and important leaders. **Students should circle the sombrero on the boy on the right.**

Page 133

For Your Information Tell students that Dr. Karenga visited Senegal, Nigeria, and Egypt on his trip to Africa. Have students find these nations on a globe or a detailed map of Africa. You might also read some of the other six rules for African American life. The other six rules are *Umoja*, which is about togetherness as a family, community, and people; *Kujichagulia*, which is about people's right to decide their own future; *Ujima*, which is about cooperation and responsibility; *Ujamaa*, which is about supporting businesses and stores operated by African Americans; *Kuumba*, which is about being creative and strengthening communities; and *Imani*, which is about believing in oneself and one's people. These may help students think of rules for all Americans. **Students' answers will vary. Suggest that volunteers share their ideas with the class.**

Page 134

Chapter Checkup Work through the Chapter Checkup with students.

Answers: 1. d **2.** c **3.** b **4.** d **5.** a **6.** a Students' answers should indicate that they make us feel that we all belong to the same country, that we are all members of the same group.

After Reading the Chapter

Ask students where their families originally came from. Write the names of these places on the chalkboard. You may wish to have students identify these places on a world map or globe. Then plan a class holiday or fair to celebrate everyone's different traditions. The celebration might include traditional foods, games, music, and crafts. Students might enjoy dressing in traditional clothing.

Social Studies
Ask students to invent a brand-new American holiday and describe it. The holiday should celebrate the huge mix of backgrounds and traditions in our country. Urge students to give their holiday a name. Be sure they explain why the holiday is important and what people do to celebrate it.

Writing
After students have finished the unit, suggest they write a description of things that make them proud to be an American.

Art
Have students work in groups to make murals that show people celebrating a holiday. Students may show in their mural the many different ways people celebrate the same holiday. Encourage students to draw upon their own experiences with the holiday when making the mural.

Final Test

The final test on the following two pages covers material from the entire book, with emphasis on material from Units 4–6.

Answers: 1. b **2.** a **3.** c **4.** c **5.** a **6.** c **7.** c **8.** a **9.** b **10.** c **11.** b **12.** c **13.** d **14.** c **15.** d **16.** c

Name _____

Final Test

Finish each sentence. Circle the letter of the correct answer.

1. A compass rose on a map helps you find
   a. the map's title.
   b. directions.
   c. the distance between two places.
   d. gardens and parks.

2. Most of the world's communities are
   a. on plains.
   b. on mountains.
   c. on hills.
   d. in valleys.

3. A suburb is
   a. a community in a rural area.
   b. a community with many tall buildings.
   c. a community near a big city.
   d. a community that relies on volunteers.

4. Consumers are people who
   a. grow or make things for sale.
   b. work to meet their needs.
   c. buy something to eat or use.
   d. work in service jobs.

5. A lawmaker's main job is to
   a. change old laws and write new ones.
   b. make sure that buildings meet safety laws.
   c. decide if laws have been broken.
   d. see that laws protecting consumers are obeyed.

6. Government leaders are chosen by the
   a. mayor.
   b. judges.
   c. voters.
   d. police.

7. People pay taxes for
   a. barbers and dry cleaners.
   b. farmers and truck drivers.
   c. school teachers and police.
   d. shopkeepers and dentists.

8. The Omaha were people of the
   a. plains.
   b. mountains.
   c. valleys.
   d. canyons.

© Harcourt Achieve Inc. All rights reserved. Steck-Vaughn Social Studies: *Living in Our Communities*   49

Name _____

Final Test (continued)

9. The Omaha met their needs and wants by
   a. making earth lodges.
   b. hunting buffalo, fishing, and farming.
   c. using horses for transportation.
   d. buying goods and services.

10. The community of Omaha, Nebraska was started by
    a. business people.
    b. farmers and cattle ranchers.
    c. pioneers.
    d. railroad workers.

11. One important industry in early Omaha was
    a. buffalo-hunting.
    b. meat-packing.
    c. unloading steamboats.
    d. fishing.

12. A time line will help you
    a. find places on a map.
    b. tell directions.
    c. see events in the order that they happened.
    d. compare numbers of things.

13. Tomorrow is part of every community's
    a. past.
    b. history.
    c. present.
    d. future.

14. The work of Congress is like the work done by a community's
    a. mayor.
    b. judge.
    c. lawmakers.
    d. police.

15. Washington, D.C., is
    a. a suburb in the eastern United States.
    b. a President of the United States.
    c. the biggest city in our country.
    d. our nation's capital.

16. Celebrating Independence Day is an important American
    a. fiesta.
    b. resource.
    c. tradition.
    d. law.

UNIT 1
Letter to Families

Date _____

Dear Family:

Throughout this school year, your child will be studying communities by using the book *Living in Our Communities*. Your child will learn that a community is a place where people live, work, and play. *Living in Our Communities* is divided into six units. The first unit, which we are completing now, shows how communities are shaped by geographical factors such as landforms and climate.

You can help your child reinforce what we study. Encourage him or her to talk to you about what we are doing. You might even want to ask your child to read aloud for you a page or two of the unit or to show you some of the pictures and maps.

Listed below are additional activities you might want to do with your child.

Thank you for your interest and support.

Sincerely,

_____

Neighborhood Walk

Take a walk together through your neighborhood and identify the kinds of buildings, businesses, and public places you see.

The Geography of Your Community

Discuss with your child what the climate is like in your community. What kind of winters and summers does it have? What kinds of landforms and vegetation characterize your community? How do the climate and landforms affect your community? Help your child make a chart that shows these things.

UNIDAD 1
Carta a las Familias

Fecha _____

Estimada familia:

   Durante este año escolar, su hijo o hija usará el libro *Living in Our Communities* para estudiar las comunidades. En este libro aprendemos que una comunidad es el lugar donde la gente vive, trabaja y disfruta. El libro *Living in Our Communities* está dividido en seis unidades. Ya casi hemos terminado la primera unidad, la cual describe como factores geográficos, como los terrenos y el clima, influyen en la formación de las comunidades.
   Usted puede ayudar a su hijo o hija a reforzar en casa lo que estamos estudiando. Para hacerlo, anímelo a conversar con usted acerca de lo que hemos estado haciendo. También puede pedirle que lea en voz alta una o dos páginas de la unidad, o que le enseñe algunas de las ilustraciones y mapas que aparecen en la misma.
   A continuación encontrará varias actividades adicionales para hacer con su hijo o hija.
   Muchas gracias por su interés y su apoyo.

Atentamente,

_____

Un paseo por el vecindario
   Den juntos un paseo por su vecindario e identifique las clases de edificios, negocios y establecimientos públicos que hay.

La geografía de su comunidad
   Converse con su hijo o hija sobre el clima de su comunidad. ¿Cómo son los inviernos y los veranos en su comunidad? ¿Qué clases de accidentes geográficos y vegetación son característicos de su comunidad? ¿Cómo afectan a su comunidad el clima y los accidentes geográficos? Ayude a su hijo o hija a preparar una gráfica que muestre todas estas cosas.

UNIT 2
Letter to Families

Date _____

Dear Family:

After studying the effects of geography on communities, we now continue by looking at different kinds of communities. In Unit 2, we studied small towns, suburbs, and cities. We looked at the differences between these kinds of communities and what life is like in each one.

Encourage your child to share with you information learned in this unit. You may also wish to talk with your child about time you or your family have spent in different kinds of communities and things about them that you liked or disliked.

Listed below are several additional activities you might want to do with your child. Thank you for your consideration and support.

Sincerely,

_____

Finding Clues

Is your community a city, a suburb, or a small town? Walk through your community and look for clues to identify what kind of community it is.

Schedule of Events

Make an itinerary of things to do in your community that would help an out-of-town guest. Include places to visit, places to eat, activities to do, and so forth.

Pen Pals

Write a letter to a friend or relative to tell about a community event. Help your child address the envelope and include his or her return address.

UNIDAD 2
Carta a las Familias

Fecha _____

Estimada familia:

Después de haber estudiado los efectos de la geografía en las comunidades, continuamos con el estudio de las distintas clases de comunidades. En la Unidad 2, estudiamos los pueblos pequeños, las áreas rurales y las ciudades. También observamos las diferencias entre las distintas clases de comunidades y los distintos estilos de vida en cada una de ellas.

Anime a su hijo o hija a compartir con usted la información que ha aprendido en esta unidad. Si gusta, converse con él o ella acerca de las ocasiones en que usted o su familia ha vivido o visitado distintas clases de comunidades, y lo que les gustó o no les gustó de cada una de ellas.

A continuación presentamos varias actividades adicionales para hacer con su hijo o hija, para enriquecer el estudio de esta unidad.

Gracias por su consideración y su apoyo.

Atentamente,

_____

Claves por todos lados

¿Es su comunidad una ciudad, parte de un área metropolitana o un pueblo pequeño? Den un paseo por su comunidad y busquen atributos que identifiquen la clase de comunidad en la que viven.

Un programa de eventos

Preparen un itinerario de cosas que un visitante podría hacer en su comunidad. Incluya lugares para visitar, restaurantes, actividades especiales, etc.

Amigo por correspondencia

Escriban una carta a un amigo o a un pariente para contarle sobre un evento de la comunidad. Ayude a su hijo o hija a poner la dirección en el sobre e incluya su dirección como remitente.

UNIT 3
Letter to Families

Date _____

Dear Family:

In our study of communities, we now turn to a consideration of the work people do there. In Unit 3, we studied how working enables people to meet their needs and wants. Then we looked at the ways that communities interact to help one another.

You can help keep your child interested in what we studied. Encourage him or her to discuss with you the goods and services your family uses. Ask your child what favorite new fact he or she learned from this unit.

Listed below are additional activities you can do with your child.

Thank you for your enthusiasm and support.

Sincerely,

_____

Needs and Wants

Go over a shopping list with your child to identify which items are needs and which are wants. Help your child number the wants in order of importance.

Goods and Services Chart

With your child think about the jobs held by friends and family members. Make a chart that gives the name of each person, what his or her job is, and whether it provides us goods or services.

Make a Flow Chart

Help your child make a flow chart of a household chore, such as setting the table or feeding a pet. Your flow chart can contain information on the production of materials used in the chore. For example, if the chore was washing dishes, you might want to have a branch showing where the water came from or something about the production of the detergent. Encourage your child to make illustrations for the steps.

UNIDAD 3
Carta a las Familias

Fecha _____

Estimada familia:

Durante nuestro estudio de las comunidades, ahora nos toca estudiar los trabajos que tiene la gente en las comunidades. En la Unidad 3, estudiamos como el trabajo permite a la gente suplir sus necesidades y preferencias. Luego observamos las distintas maneras en que las comunidades trabajan juntas para ayudarse entre sí.

Usted puede ayudar a mantener a su hijo o hija interesado en lo que estamos estudiando. Anímelo a que le cuente sobre los bienes y servicios que usa su familia. Pregúntele qué es lo que más le gusta de lo que ha aprendido en esta unidad.

A continuación presentamos varias actividades adicionales que puede hacer con su hijo o hija.

Gracias por su entusiasmo y su apoyo.

Atentamente,

_____

Necesidades: ¿sí o no?

Repase con su hijo o hija una lista de compras para identificar los artículos que son verdaderas necesidades y los que no lo son. Ayúdele a numerar en orden de importancia los artículos que no son verdaderas necesidades.

Tabla de bienes y servicios

Piense con su hijo o hija acerca de las ocupaciones que tienen sus amigos y los miembros de su familia. Preparen una tabla que incluya el nombre de cada persona, el tipo de trabajo que hace y si esa ocupación proporciona bienes o servicios.

Un diagrama de flujo

Ayude a su hijo o hija a preparar un diagrama de flujo para un quehacer cualquiera, como poner la mesa o darle de comer a una mascota. El diagrama de flujo puede contener información acerca de la producción de los materiales que se usan para cada tarea. Por ejemplo, si la tarea es lavar los platos, pueden hacer que una rama del diagrama muestre de dónde viene el agua que usarían o algo sobre la producción del detergente. Anime a su hijo o hija a ilustrar los distintos pasos del diagrama.

UNIT 4
Letter to Families

Date _____

Dear Family:

Our next topic in studying communities is learning how they are run. In Unit 4, which we are now completing, we began by thinking about the people who run communities. Next, we looked at the rules and laws that help communities function fairly and smoothly. Finally, we considered the services that communities provide.

There are several ways to reinforce what we have studied. Encourage your child to read aloud to you a page or two of the unit or to show you some of the pictures and maps. Discuss what your child knows about the leaders of your community and the rules and laws that govern it.

Listed below are additional activities you might want to do with your child.

Thank you for your continuing interest and support.

Sincerely,

_____

Who's the Boss?

Identify the leaders in your community. Look for newspaper articles about the leaders and their positions on current issues. You may want to select one leader and help your child make a scrapbook about that person and his or her activities in the community over the last few months.

S.O.S.

Go over the procedures for what to do in an emergency in your community (for example, calling 911 and so forth). Make a list of important phone numbers and hang it by the telephone. You might act out several potential situations, as well.

Improving Your Community

With your child, come up with some things that you think need improving in your community. Should there be a stop light at a certain busy corner? What about building a community pool or passing a stronger law against littering? Select one improvement and find out something about the procedures necessary to bring it about.

UNIDAD 4
Carta a las Familias

Fecha _____

Estimada familia:

Nuestro siguiente tema en el estudio de las comunidades consiste en aprender como se administran las comunidades. En la Unidad 4, que ahora estamos completando, comenzamos a pensar acerca de las personas que administran las comunidades. Luego, observamos las reglas y las leyes que ayudan a que las comunidades funcionen bien. Finalmente, consideramos los servicios que proporcionan las comunidades.

Hay varias maneras de reforzar lo que hemos estudiado. Anime a su hijo o hija a que le lea en voz alta una o dos de las páginas de la unidad, o que le muestre algunos de los dibujos y mapas de la unidad. Converse sobre lo que sabe su hijo o hija sobre los líderes de su comunidad y sobre las reglas y leyes que la gobiernan.

A continuación aparecen varias actividades adicionales que puede hacer con su hijo o hija.

Gracias por su continuo interés y su apoyo.

Atentamente,

_____

¿Quién es el jefe?

Identifiquen a los líderes de su comunidad. Busquen en el periódico artículos acerca de ellos y de lo que piensan acerca de situaciones de la actualidad. Si quiere, escoja un líder y ayude a su hijo o hija a preparar un álbum de recortes de esa persona y de sus actividades en la comunidad durante los últimos meses.

S.O.S.

Repase con su hijo o hija los procedimientos que se deben llevar a cabo durante una emergencia en su comunidad (por ejemplo, llamar al 911). Preparen una lista con números telefónicos importantes y cuelguen la lista al lado del teléfono. También puede que quieran representar varias situaciones de emergencia.

Para mejorar la comunidad

Piense con su hijo o hija en varias cosas que creen que se necesitan para mejorar su comunidad. ¿Debería haber un semáforo en cierta esquina con mucho tráfico? ¿Deberían construir una piscina pública o pasar una ley más estricta contra quienes boten basura en la calle? Escojan una de las mejores ideas y averigüen acerca de los procedimientos que se deben llevar a cabo para hacer la idea realidad.

UNIT 5
Letter to Families

Date _____

Dear Family:

Now we turn our attention to the history of communities—the way they change over time. In Unit 5, we looked at a typical American Indian community in the early 1800s. Then we studied the arrival of the pioneers. Finally, we examined some causes of growth and change in communities.

Encourage your child to show you some of the pictures and maps in this unit. You may wish to ask what he or she has learned about changes in your own community. If there is a local historical museum, you may want to visit it with your child.

Listed below are additional activities you might want to do with your child.

Thank you for your continuing support of our studies.

Sincerely,

_____

Changing Sites

With your child select a building or site such as a park or school that you know has changed over the years. Try to find some pictures of the building or site that reflect the changes it has gone through. Help your child make a poster about it using pictures. You could add photographs of yourself and your child at the times when the changes took place.

Interview an Older Resident

Help your child interview a senior citizen who has lived in your community for most of his or her life. You might contact a local nursing home if you don't have an appropriate friend or relative. Before the interview, come up with some questions about your community's past you'd like the interview subject to answer.

UNIDAD 5
Carta a las Familias

Fecha _____

Estimada familia:

Ahora concentramos nuestros estudios en la historia de las comunidades; es decir, en la manera en que las comunidades cambian a través del tiempo. En la Unidad 5, observamos una comunidad típica de los indios americanos durante los primeros años del siglo dieciocho y luego estudiamos la llegada de los pioneros. Hacia el final, examinamos algunas de las causas del crecimiento y de los cambios de las comunidades.

Anime a su hijo o hija a mostrarle algunos de los dibujos y mapas de esta unidad. Si lo desea, pregúntele sobre lo que ha aprendido acerca de los cambios en su propia comunidad. Si hay un museo histórico local pueden visitarlo juntos.

A continuación hay varias actividades adicionales para hacer con su hijo o hija. Gracias por su continuo apoyo en nuestros estudios.

Atentamente,

_____

Lugares que cambian

Junto con su hijo o hija escojan un edificio u otro lugar, como un parque o una escuela, que usted sepa ha cambiado a través de los años. Trate de encontrar algunos dibujos de ese lugar que reflejen los cambios por los que ha pasado. Ayude a su hijo o hija a hacer un cartel con ilustraciones del lugar que escogieron. También podrían añadir fotografías de usted mismo y de su hijo o hija de la época en que ocurrió cada cambio.

Entrevista de un vecino mayor

Ayude a su hijo o hija a entrevistar a un vecino ya mayor que haya vivido en su comunidad por la mayor parte de su vida. Puede ponerse en contacto con un ancianato si no tiene un amigo o pariente al que pueda entrevistar. Antes de la entrevista, preparen algunas preguntas sobre el pasado de su comunidad que les gustaría que contestara esa persona.

UNIT 6
Letter to Families

Date _____

Dear Family:

We now look outward to see some things that the varied communities of the United States share. During our study of Unit 6, we visited a community important to us all, Washington, D.C. Then we studied the way communities celebrate, both across the nation and within different communities.

You can help your child personalize what we have studied in this unit. Encourage him or her to talk to you about what we have learned. Discuss with your child what holiday he or she likes celebrating best and why.

Listed below are a few additional activities to do with your child.

Thank you for your continuing enthusiasm and support.

Sincerely,

_____

Washington News

Watch or listen to a national news broadcast each day for a week. Or check a national newspaper or weekly news magazine. Help your child make a list of the events that happened in Washington, D.C. during that week. Discuss the effects that these events might have on your community.

Let's Celebrate

Go over your plans for an American holiday or your own ethnic celebration. Discuss any special family traditions associated with the event.

Holidays

Help your child make a list of the holidays that the people of your community celebrate. Mark the holidays *N* (national), *C* (community), or *G* (religious or ethnic group) depending on who celebrates them. You may want to write the holiday names on a calendar and add the appropriate letter and a sentence telling something about each holiday.

UNIDAD 6
Carta a las Familias

Fecha _____

Estimada familia:

Ahora vamos a mirar más allá de nuestra comunidad, para ver algunas de las cosas que comparten las distintas comunidades de los Estados Unidos. Durante nuestros estudios en la Unidad 6, hemos visitado una comunidad importante para todos nosotros: Washington, D. C. Luego estudiamos las maneras en que las comunidades llevan a cabo sus celebraciones, tanto para fiestas nacionales como para celebraciones locales.

Usted puede ayudar a su hijo o hija a personalizar lo que hemos estudiado en esta unidad. Anímelo a conversar con usted sobre lo que hemos tratado en clase. Luego conversen sobre un día de fiesta en particular que le guste celebrar a él o a ella y las razones por las cuales le gusta.

A continuación presentamos varias actividades adicionales para hacer con su hijo o hija.

Gracias por su continuo entusiasmo y su apoyo.

Atentamente,

_____

Las noticias de Washington

Todos los días durante una semana, observen o escuchen un noticiero nacional, o lean un periódico nacional o una revista semanal de noticias. Ayude a su hijo o hija a preparar una lista de los eventos que suceden en Washington, D. C. durante esa semana. Conversen sobre los efectos que estos eventos puedan tener en su comunidad.

¡A celebrar!

Repasen sus planes para un día de fiesta que se celebra en los Estados Unidos o para una celebración tradicional de otro país. Conversen sobre la manera en que su familia celebra dicho evento.

Días de fiesta

Ayude a su hijo o hija a preparar una lista de los días de fiesta que se celebran en su su comunidad. Indique los días de fiesta con una *N* (Nacional), una *C* (Comunidad) o una *G* (Grupo religioso o étnico) dependiendo de quienes los celebran. También pueden escribir los nombres de los días de fiesta en un calendario, añadir la letra apropiada y una oración que diga algo sobre cada día de fiesta.

Name

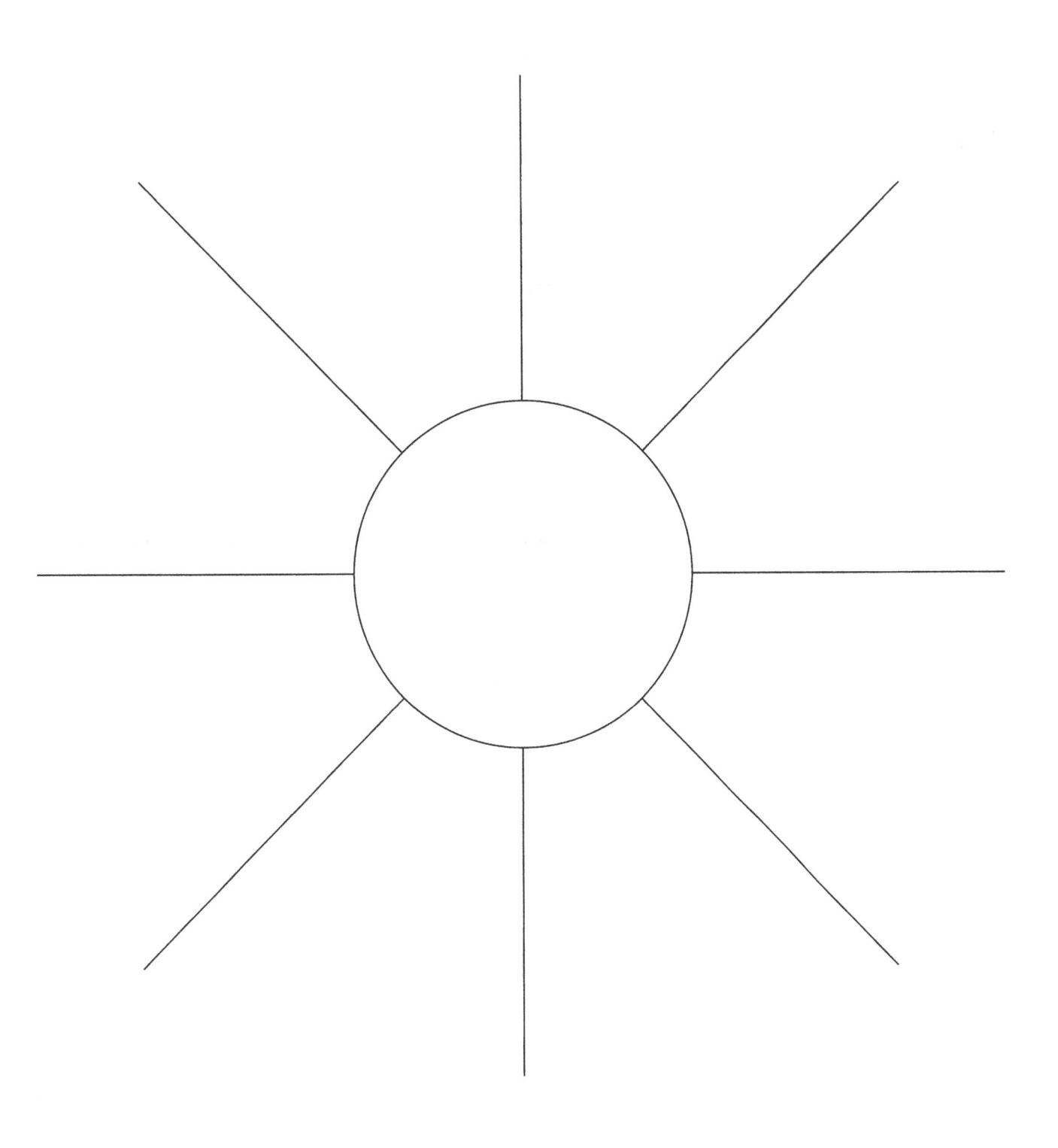

GRAPHIC ORGANIZER
Concept Web

Name _____

GRAPHIC ORGANIZER
Cause and Effect

Cause →

Effect 1

Effect 2

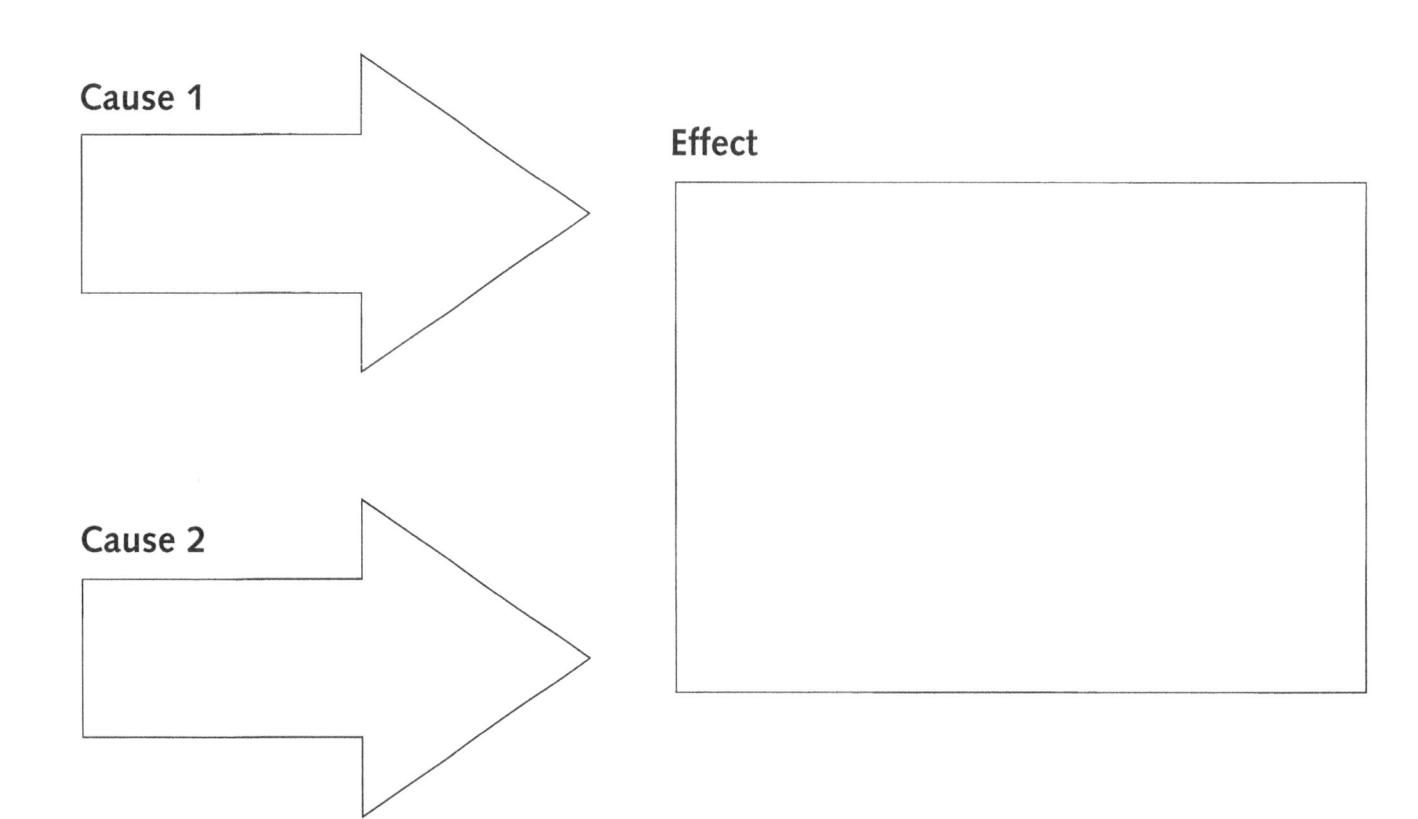

Cause 1 →

Cause 2 →

Effect